From the Inside Out
Reviving the Faith

From Prison to Pulpit/From Sinner to Saint

An Autobiography of Saving Grace
Rev. David L Dillard
5/12/2023

Showing how faith in God, Obedience and a desire to walk right in all of life's circumstances will result in God's favor over your life. Even when you're unfaithful and afraid God is always faithful and true!

Copyright © 2025

All Right Reserved.

Contents

PROLOGUE 1

PART ONE INTRODUCTION 3

THE BEGINNING 6

PART TWO NOBODY TOLD ME THE ROAD WOULD BE EASY 21

PART THREE PLEASE BE PATIENT WITH ME 32

PART FOUR ANGELS 41

PART FIVE "…BUT I DON'T BELIEVE HE BROUGHT ME THIS FAR TO LEAVE ME" 54

PART SIX "IT WON'T BE LONG TILL WE'LL BE LEAVING HERE; IT WON'T BE LONG TILL WE'LL BE GOING HOME." 62

PART SEVEN RESTORATIONS 70

PART EIGHT LIVING ON THE OUTSIDE 2010 TO PRESENT (2023) 80

PART NINE CONCLUSION 89

PROLOGUE

As I began to look back over the journals and notes that I have kept over the years and the many ups and downs life has brought my way I started to realize that my life, the good and the bad, has been a testimony to the goodness of God. I have spent nearly half of my life in prison beginning at the age of 17. I have attempted to live those years behind bars for God, a Christian life though often not feeling like a Christian.

You see even though I was praying daily, studying God's Word, teaching Bible studies, and witnessing to others about how good God was, I was also smoking cigarettes for much of the nearly 26 years I was in prison; gambling, and on a few occasions fighting. It was only near the last five years of my incarceration that I realized that even in my unfaithfulness that God was still faithful to me. God begin to show me that whereas I was judging myself and my relationship with Him on my feelings, which changed on a daily basis, (and often on an hourly or minute by minute basis), and also on some of the things that I was doing, He, God that is, was looking at my heart. Now allow me to qualify that. This is not to say that the wrong things that I did were justified but that God was not "judging" me for what I was doing but instead was looking down on me in the mercy and grace that was brought on by His Son's blood sacrifice on Calvary's cross. At the same time I was in life's class of sanctification. I was brought under conviction each and every time I did something wrong; in other words every cigarette I put in my mouth brought about guilt. I attempted to quit probably over a hundred times during those years but it wasn't until I learned that I could do nothing on my own and turned the cigarette's over to God that He took the desire away from me. The

Apostle Paul says "For the flesh desires what is contrary to the Spirit, and the Spirit what is contrary to the flesh. They are in conflict with each other, so that you are not to do whatever you want." (Galatians 5:17). There was not a day that went by during the time I was incarcerated that I didn't have to fall on my knees and seek forgiveness and still today nearly sixteen years since my release I often find myself on my knees seeking God's forgiveness.

Anyway, this book, or missive as I call it, is about the goodness of God in the small and the big areas of life. It's sort of an autobiography of the ups and downs of Christian growth in the life of a teenage kid who grew up in prison. Memories of how good God has been in my life. If you are looking just for a good crime novel about the crimes I committed, how big and bad I thought I was before incarceration, while incarcerated or after incarceration you might as well put this book down. This is about how God has worked in my life with the hope that it will give hope to someone else struggling with their faith in God, questioning their salvation every time they fall. I want people to know that if your heart is right with God then He will bring the rest of you around. Finally, there is lots of scripture quotation in this writing as it is my belief that "the word of God is alive and active. Sharper than any double-edged sword, it penetrates even to dividing soul and spirit, joints and marrow; it judges the thoughts and attitudes of the heart." I hope this journey of mine encourages and bless.

PART ONE
INTRODUCTION

HE BROUUGHT ME FROM A MIGHTY LONG WAY

"However, I consider my life worth nothing to me; my only aim is to finish the race and complete the task the Lord Jesus has given me--the task of testifying to the good news of God's grace." Acts 20:24 (NIV)

I have attempted to start this missive on several occasions but I could never decide just where to start. As I finally prayed and ask God if it was in His will for me to write it, that He would guide my mind, heart, and hand in doing so, the Holy Spirit brought to my remembrance God's words to the Apostle John in Revelations: "I am Alpha and Omega, the beginning and the ending, saith the Lord, which is, and which was, and which is to come, the Almighty." Rev. 1:8, 22:13. (KJV)

This was not to be a missive or writing just about me, my conversion, the time I spent in prison, how I was released, or what I have done since my release. It is to be a "testimony" of God's salvation, protection, deliverance, and ministry throughout my life. You see the beginning and the ending are all about God and how He uses the least of us to accomplish His will. 1 Corinthians 1:27.

I once read an illustrative report from a church search committee that was looking for a new pastor. It illustrated how many of the churches today think when trying to pick God's leaders on their own. The candidates were as follows:

Adam: Good man but he has problems with his wife. One reference we had on him said that he and his wife enjoyed walking nude in the woods; Noah: Former pastor of one-hundred twenty years with no converts. Prone to unrealistic building projects; Joseph: A big thinker, but a braggart; believes in dream interpretation and he has a prison record; Moses: A modest and meek man, but a poor communicator, he even stutters at times. Sometimes he blows his stack and acts rashly in business meetings. Some even say he left an earlier church over a murder charge; Deborah: One word---female; David: The most promising leader of all until we discovered the affair he had with his neighbors wife.

There were many more: Solomon was a great preacher but had serious women problems; Elijah was prone to depression and collapses under pressure; Hosea was a tender loving pastor but people could never handle his wife's occupation; Jonah told us he was swallowed up by a great fish that later spit him out. We just hung up on him; John said he is a Baptist, but he doesn't dress like one. He may actually be too Pentecostal as he tends to lift both his hands in the air to worship when he gets excited; Peter has a bad temper and it's even said that he cursed once. He's a loose cannon; Paul is a fascinating preacher, however he is short on tact, unforgiving with young ministers, harsh, and has been known to preach all night; Timothy, well he's too young.

The final two candidates were the most promising of all and of the two we found the one we wanted.

Jesus: Has had popular times and His church once actually grew to over 5000. He managed to offend them all though and, His church dwindled down to just twelve people. He seldom stays in one place and of course he is single, can't seem to find a wife.

But the final candidate and our choice is one Judas: His reference is solid; he's conservative and has good connections; he knows how to handle money. We have already invited him to preach this Sunday!

"But the LORD said to Samuel, "Don't judge by his appearance or height, for I have rejected him. The LORD doesn't see things the way you see them. People judge by outward appearance, but the LORD looks at the heart." 1 Samuel 16:7 (NLT)

THE BEGINNING

"O come, let us worship and bow down: let us kneel before the LORD our maker." Psalms 95:6(KJV); "And Elijah went up to the top of Carmel; and he cast himself down upon the earth, and put his face between his knees;" 1 Kings 18:42 (KJV); "And Moses made haste, and bowed his head toward the earth, and worshipped" Exod. 34:8 (KJV).

It began on bent knees in a small apartment in Cedartown GA., about nineteen miles from Rome GA., and sixty-five or so miles northwest of Atlanta.

The first work of the Holy Spirit is conviction; conviction results in humility; both conviction and humility are the result of hearing the powerful Word of God. "How then shall they call on him in whom they have not believed? And how shall they believe in him of whom they have not heard? And how shall they hear without a preacher?" (Romans 10:14, KJV). "So then faith *cometh* by hearing, and hearing by the word of God" (Romans 10:17, KJV).

As I listened to Billy Graham on the TV the Holy Spirit brought about conviction in my life and as a result I humbled myself in front of my sofa, falling on my knees and seeking God's forgiveness and guidance. Not only did I want salvation I needed to know which way God wanted me to go. I was lost, tired and more than anything else lonely. I felt like I had no one in the world who understood me. I had done some bad things and my sins were brought before me like a movie running through my mind. I was scared. I truly believe that my death from this world and in my sins was at that time upon me... in fact I know that it was. Had I not heeded the Holy Spirits calling on this night I would have died in my sins bound for hell. But God's grace and mercy…

As I knelt and prayed and begged God's forgiveness the Holy Spirit fell on me as never before; as I had only seen it fall on others and wondered if they were just acting. Tears poured from my eyes and I begin to tremble all over. My prayer for forgiveness changed from a prayer of petition to a prayer of praise as I found myself joyfully thanking God and acknowledging His power and presence; praying scriptures that I had learned in Sunday school as a child, whole Psalms coming back to my remembrance. Along with the scriptures and Psalms came revelations of their meaning that revealed God Himself to me for the first time in my life. I begin to speak in an unknown tongue and though I couldn't tell you at that time what I was saying somehow in my spirit I knew. The words of God to Ananais concerning the Apostle Paul reverberated throughout my mind: "For I will shew him how great things he must suffer for my name's sake" (Acts 9:16, KJV). As my prayer mingled between the language of men and the unknown tongues one phrase kept coming through; and though my spirit seemed to have a dread of that phrase I had no power to cease or stop my spirit from praying it… "Lord your will be done, Lord your will be done, Lord your will be done…"

I could see God's presence, I could feel God's presence, and I could hear Him. All of my senses were in line and tuned entirely to and on God. Though I have felt the presence of God on many occasions since then I have never felt it again as I did on this occasion or to this extent. Finally, peace. The peace promised by our Lord, "Peace I leave with you, my peace I give unto you: not as the world giveth, give I unto you. Let not your heart be troubled, neither let it be afraid" (John 14:27, KJV).

"Only be careful, and watch yourselves closely so that you do not forget the things your eyes have seen or let them fade from your heart as long as you live. Teach them to your children and their children after them." Deut. 4:9 (KJV)

Surreal; like in a dream. As I sat in the Fulton County Superior Court before the Honorable Judge Clearance Cooper, I felt no fear, no happiness or joy, no hate, no guilt or remorse. Nothing that I could describe except, it didn't feel real. I heard the people talking and I knew they were talking about me. Whether or not they would seek the death penalty; was his statement to police voluntary or not, and having a "Denno" hearing to find out. Though I was there and heard everything, somehow I was not there; it was like being in a dream.

I had sat in the county jail for months before finally going to trial so I don't really think I was in a state of shock. I knew I was facing a murder charge and what the possible consequences were. I knew the evidence they had against me, the most damning being the statement I had given to the police myself.

While in the county jail I had begun to do what most all people in jail do who are facing serious charges. I began reading the Bible and praying constantly. Everybody telling you a "special" scripture to read that guaranteed that it would get you off with the most popular ones being the twenty-third and thirty-fifth Psalms.

All the religious folks that came into the jail to minister to the inmates had a special message that offered Gods protection from whatever you were facing. And even though I was raised by a Christian mother and considered myself a Christian at that time, I went to all the different services, except for Islam, looking for a way out. I visited the Jehovah Witnesses as they were the most persistent in their pursuit. My mind and spirit couldn't get around the idea that Jesus and God were not the same; that there is no physical hell or Holy Spirit. If there was no Holy Spirit then what had happened to me in the apartment in Cedartown? I also tried the Catholic services and even though they taught Jesus Christ my mind couldn't seem to grasp the ideal of penance and praying to the Virgin Mary. I would later during my incarceration look into Buddhism, Islam, Mormonism, Satanism and atheist-ism and though I thought I was, I was not looking for God. I was looking for a way to escape punishment. I didn't want to go to prison for the rest of my life as two of my brothers were already serving multiple life sentences. I had been to visit them many times and heard the horror stories of what went on in prison. I also found out while in the county jail that my girlfriend was pregnant. Man I did not want to go to jail!

Daily I sat and listened to the stories about the "hanging judges" and who had got this amount of time and who had beat their charge or been offered a deal. I listened to the talk about how good or great this or that lawyer was and how the public defenders, who represented those who couldn't afford an attorney, also worked for the state and just wanted to get all their client to plead guilty. Even knowing my momma and daddy had no money I begged, pleaded and cried for them to get me an attorney. I didn't care who he was as long as he wasn't a state appointed lawyer.

As I look back over that entire time in the county jail I think about the children of Israel when they were released from slavery in Egypt. After seeing and experiencing the ten plagues performed while in Egypt, and then the parting of the Red Sea, water from a rock, and all the other God present moments, they soon forgot, begin to complain and look at circumstances and to seek other god's than the one they knew had rescued them (Exodus chapters 7-17 and chapter 32). Even today I hear people talking about if they had lived back then, seen and heard God like the Israelites, that there is no way they would have forgotten. But we forget every day. Every time we do something not pleasing to God or against His will we forget. The biggest way we forget is when we don't trust or have faith in God in the midst of life's everyday struggles. "But without faith it is impossible to please God: for he that cometh to God must believe that He is, and that He is a rewarder of them that diligently seek Him" (Hebrews 11:6, KJV).

While in the county jail my mind seem to put the experience that I had in the apartment living room in Cedartown, the very presence of God that I had felt, into a corner of forgetfulness. I was looking in every direction, listening to everybody, trusting everything but God. I can just imagine the Israelites from back in Exodus today saying, if I had a Savior that I knew had hung, bleed and died for my sins and if I could feel and know the everyday experience of the indwelling Holy Spirit I'd never forget. I think at some point in life we all forget. But like the song writer wrote "We fall down but we get up" (Written by Bob Carlisle, performed by Pastor Donnie McClurkin).

"Train up a child in the way he should go: and when he is old he will not depart from it." Proverbs 22:6. (KJV)

I was raised Fire Baptize Holiness (FBH). The strictest denomination that I know of; an unbending, unyielding religion; sort of a resemblance to the biblical Pharisees, or at least the particular church I attended was this way. No jewelry was allowed, no wedding bands, watches, ear rings, bracelets or necklaces; the women wore dresses or skirts down to the ankle; no contact between women and men of adult age or teenage years unless they were married to each other.

We had Sunday school that begin at seven thirty Sunday morning and went until four Sunday evening; at seven thirty Sunday evening we had worship service. Tuesday and Friday evenings was also worship service nights. Worship service rarely ended before one in the morning and many of nights going until three or four in the morning. Wednesday nights was bible study; Thursday night was choir practice for adults and Saturday afternoon and evenings was choir practice for young children and young adults. All of these services lasted until the "Spirit" released them or until you got it right. Also on Saturday was car washing and breakfast and dinner plates sold from the church kitchen. All women that didn't work on Saturday were expected to be there all day (All day being from six in the morning until nine or ten at night).

There were many dues to be paid; Sunday school dues, choir dues, children dues, young adult dues, adult dues. Then there were separate tithes and offerings required. Parents had to pay their children's dues until they were out of school or working.

Members were not allowed to go to or visit other churches for any reason without prior permission from the pastor. You couldn't even attend another family member's funeral at another church or funeral home without permission. There were other FBH churches but we were taught that we were the only "saved" congregation. When we went to FBH yearly convention we could not "amen" another preacher or even the Bishop unless prior permission was given.

If you didn't learn your Sunday school lesson by Sunday or didn't study or couldn't answer a question during Sunday school you were whipped or beat. It didn't matter your age this started from the time you could talk and comprehend a little all the way through your adult life; the same with learning the words to the songs in the choir or not paying your dues on time. If the children dues were not paid both child and parent were punished. This was the only form of church or Christianity I knew. My momma always told me she got saved and joined the church when she was pregnant with me. So my sister and I were both raised in this church. My two oldest brothers were members of Church of God in Christ and constantly kept trying to get my mother to leave her church or at least to visit their church. But like me and my sister my mother was afraid that if we left this church we would instantly die and go to hell or some other horrible fate would befall us.

Unlike in most of today's churches, the message was not based on "For God so loved the world, that He gave His only begotten Son, that whosoever believeth in Him should not perish, but have everlasting life" (John 3:16, KJV); it was not based on God's love, grace and mercy. The message was always if you don't obey and get saved you're going to die and burn in hell fire and condemnation forever and ever and you were probably going to die sooner rather than later. Salvation was based on your fear of God and obedience to the church rules which were ordained by God. If you left this church you were automatically condemned.

Salvation was not as easy as "That if thou shalt confess with thy mouth the Lord Jesus, and shalt believe in thine heart that God hath raised Him from the dead, thou shalt be saved" (Romans 10:9, KJV). No, salvation was a process that more times than not required years of pleading with God on the alter in the church to "save me Lord" repeated over and over again each night during service for a minimum of an hour and most church nights more like two or three hours. You were only saved when the Holy Ghost fell on you and you spoke in tongues. After you got "saved" this process was repeated for the second phase which was sanctification, "sanctify me Lord" and the third phase "glory, glory, glory..." which was to be filled with the Holy Ghost. As I said earlier the whole process usually took a couple of years or longer. I knew people who had been on "the alter" for over three years and yet still in the first stage of getting saved. One thing was for sure; when you finally got up you knew you were saved.

But there was what I considered the good in the church. Every year they took the kids to Disney World in Florida. We also got to go to Callaway Gardens in Pine Mountain Georgia every year and the annual trip to the FBH convention in Greenville South Carolina was fun.

Nearly all of the members in the church rode in nice looking Cadillac's, Mercedes Benz, or BMW's as the pastor owned a car lot and allowed members to pay for these vehicles with food stamps or by working for his construction company. Of course you never really owned the cars yourself. We young guys couldn't wait until we turned sixteen and got a job so that we could get one of these nice cars. Also many of the members stayed in the pastors apartment complex's or houses.

But the most important and valuable thing that I got from this church was the Word of God. Not necessarily the true Spirit of the Word but the letter or mental education of the Word itself: the Bible. Paul said, "But what does it matter? The important thing is that in every way, whether from false motives or true, Christ is preached. And because of this I rejoice. Yes, and I will continue to rejoice" (Philippians 1:18, NIV).

By the age of thirteen I could recite all sixty six books of the bible in order; I knew the twelve tribes of Israel; the ten plagues brought on the Egyptian's; the first, fifteenth, twenty third, one hundred, and one hundred and twenty first Psalms by hard; I knew the old testament was broken down into the Pentateuch (or law), historical books, poetry, and major and minor prophets; I knew the order of the creation, about the flood, and much more; I could recite the twelve disciples, the beatitudes, the Lord's prayer and the fruits of the spirit. I knew the story of Jesus life and death from the point of all four of the Gospels and of Paul's conversion and life.

My mama and the church also taught us to fear and respect all grown folks and authority. "Yes maam, yes sir, no maam, and no sir were mandatory. If you sinned or broke the law you were going to hell. I didn't like getting whipped or beat so I learned fast and well.

Later in life, during my trial and incarceration (and many other life's trials) it was this learned Word that brought me through. "For the word of God is quick, and powerful, and sharper than any two-edged sword, piercing even to the dividing asunder of soul and spirit, and of the joints and marrow, and is a discerner of the thoughts and intents of the heart" (Hebrews 4:12, KJV).

It was this Word that was drilled and beat into me as a child that would later in life save my life; it was this Word that brought me to my knees in Cedartown Georgia to confess my sins and submit my life to Christ. As I think about those days when the Word was being forced into me and later during my conversion in Cedartown the scripture comes to mind "For it is written, As I live, saith the Lord, every knee shall bow to me, and every tongue shall confess to God." Romans 14:11 (KJV)

"Beloved, believe not every spirit, but try the spirits whether they are of God: because many false prophets are gone out into the world" (1 John 4:1, KJV).

I've mentioned that my sister and I were raised in the FBH church and that my two oldest brothers were members of Church of God in Christ. But there are two more brothers that attended no church at all. Both of these brothers were in prison during my conversion. In prison for murder and, both sentenced to multiple life sentences and years and years added on to that. Never to be released. The older of these two brothers, Jeffery, was my hero and idol. Jeffery had been in the Marine Corps and was a martial arts teacher. I was so fascinated when he got out of the Marines and would impress me and my friends busting bricks and wooden boards with his hands. That aura of danger about him was something right out of the movies to me. I even thought he had the greatest and best looking family in the world, his wife in my opinion was the prettiest lady I knew and his three daughters were perfect in my view. I wanted a life just like him when I got older. Even when Jeffery when to prison I visited as often as I could to hear the stories he would tell me about what went on in prison. He was always a great story teller.

It was these two brothers eventually that caused both me and my mother to leave the only church I had ever known and the only church that I thought was going to heaven. My sister, being a little bit more independent than both me and my mother, had married at the age of sixteen and left the church when they refused to except her husband's salvation and claims to be a preacher. They even prophesied that he was gay. This prophecy actually turned out to be true as two children and a few years later my sister caught him in bed with a man in her house. She left him and, after I was incarcerated for several years he too was convicted, of molesting little boys in a church he had started. I ran into him on numerous occasions in prison.

After I left the church myself it was prophesied that I would be following in my brother's footsteps and end up in prison for the rest of my life; yet another prophecy that came true. I remember going to the church to pick my mother up, and one of my aunts coming out to tell me that the spirit had told the church that I was on my way to prison. This worried me quite a bit as I was still in the grips of fear from leaving the church. However, another prophecy that had come through the church about me before I left, and that was totally unfounded and untrue and was part of the reason I left, gave me some confidence that not all their prophecies were true. I had been called up in "counsel meeting" which was the churches form of disciplinary court, held on one Friday out of the month, and where anybody who had "sinned" , which included not paying church dues, being out of church without excuse, visiting another church without permission, not learning a Sunday school lesson or various other offenses were punished. Punishment usually included being slapped around by the Pastor or beat by deacons. In this particular council meeting I was told that I was doing drugs, missing church to party and was gay. Even though I had paid all my dues and knew all of my Sunday school assignments I had missed several services and choir practices. I also had bought a car that was not bought from the Pastor and I had no girlfriend in the church as all the other young teenage boys had.

In actuality I was a nerd; straight A student; never touched drugs or alcohol. I had two jobs after school and on the weekends, which is why I was missing some services and choir practices.

I was a sixteen years old and I had a girlfriend who I had brought to the church once, but seeing the "shouting" "falling out" and speaking in tongues, the church had both frightened and amused her. She refused to come back. My daddy hated the church and the Pastor with a passion. He had been locked up on numerous occasions for kicking the church doors open at two or three in the morning looking for my mother while service was going on. To this day I don't know how or why he was never sent to prison. I don't even remember him ever going to court. But it was my dad who had co-signed with me to get a car loan and there was no way he was going to allow me to buy a car from the church, no matter how much I begged.

At the time I was brought up in counsel meeting and told that I was doing drugs and gay, both my brothers had broken out of prison and we had them hid in an apartment in Atlanta. Looking back in retrospect, after personally being incarcerated in Georgia's prison I can't fathom how they managed to escape. They broke out of different prisons within a week of each other. The week after Jeffery had broken out we visited my other brother, Wayne, with the message that he was not to try the same thing as we were sure he was being watched closely. When we got home from the prison that Saturday evening we were met by police and prison officials who busted open the trunk of mama's car thinking that Wayne had left the prison with us. He had broken out as soon as we left the visitation room.

Anyway, after leaving the council meeting I went straight to the apartment that my two escaped brothers were hiding out in. I informed them of the prophesied allegation against me assuring them that none of it was true. While they laughed and joked my insides were churning with fear that God was about to do a terrible thing in my life.

I had just got paid from two of my jobs that Friday and had money in my pockets. My brothers convinced me that since the church had accused me of doing drugs and alcohol already, I might as well do it. My brother Jeffery assured me that I was never going back to that church and if anybody had a problem with it he'd deal with them and protect me from any retribution. So with my pay check that was meant for my church dues I paid for marijuana and alcohol. And while drunk and high for the first time in my life I also lost my virginity to a young lady on the living room floor while my brothers, their wives and my sister looked and cheered me on. It would be nearly thirty years later before I set foot into that church again. My mama was heartbroken that the last of her children, and her baby at that had left the church. She was certain in her mind though that she had brought us up right and that with constant prayer for us we would come back. It would only be a few more years before she too would leave the church.

My brothers would be out on escape for over a year before they were caught. They eventually left Georgia and went to Philadelphia and only got caught when they came back to Georgia. Before they left for Philadelphia though, I was a regular marijuana and wine lover. A few days before they left I learned another lesson.

I drove them to a business establishment. While they went in to buy some things I waited in the car. A few minutes later they came out carrying small bags. I thought nothing of it. I simply drove off. As we got further down the road they opened the bags and poured the contents onto the car seat next to me. Money! They had robbed the place. The lesson they told me was that you should always act normal and never panic or draw attention. A few days later they would be gone, sent to Philadelphia Pennsylvania by my daddy.

I was left with my sister's section eight apartment that had been hiding out in (my sister had moved to Cedartown with her husband). I was miserable and lonely. I regularly visited my sister in Cedartown with her husband and two children. She and I were best friends and weed smoking buddies now.

It wouldn't be long before me and a couple of my buddies were robbing folks with me teaching them the lessons my brothers had taught me.

After my brothers were caught and sent back to prison my mother was told by the church that she could not visit them or communicate with them anymore. Nor was she to have anything to do with me or my sister unless we came back to the church. "This is what the spirit had commanded." This was more than my mother could bear. She disappeared one day and we went looking for her. I found her some miles away from home walking and crying. We had to admit her to a mental hospital because she was torn between her children and her church and didn't know what to do. After she was released from the hospital she didn't attend church anywhere for over a year. She did continue to visit my brothers in prison though. She was waiting each and every day for God to kill her for leaving and disobeying the church. My oldest brothers eventually convinced her to come to church with them and she soon joined Church of God in Christ. She never returned to her old church during her life. My mother's sisters who still attended this church put out the word that my mother was a heathen and even went so far as to proclaim that she had become a witch. Her only hope was to return to the church before God destroyed her.

PART TWO
NOBODY TOLD ME THE ROAD WOULD BE EASY

"And the peace of God, which passeth all understanding, shall keep your hearts and minds through Christ Jesus (Philippians 4:7, KJV).

"I sentence you to serve the rest of your natural born life in a Georgia Penitentiary, plus twenty two additional years." As stated earlier I was numb and yet somehow at peace when I heard these words come out of the judge's mouth. Again, I don't think I was in any kind of shock. I knew this was coming. I was not afraid of these words nor what they meant. God had actually given me a peace that even today is hard to explain.

The two things about this trial that most bothered me at that time was the hurt that it caused my parents and the words of the district attorney in his closing arguments: "this man is a menace to society." There was no victim's family present during this whole ordeal but these word's cut through me like a hot knife through butter and would haunt me throughout the years in prison.

As I look back over my life I think my parents did a great job in raising us. It most definitely was not their fault in any way the choices that my brothers and I had made to do wrong. Both my parents were hard working folk. My mama went back to school in her thirties and got a high school diploma and to college to get her associates degree. She worked two and three jobs to make sure that my sister and I had everything we both needed and wanted. My daddy never even saw his paychecks. He worked for the railroad and later for the same construction company for over forty years. My mama went and picked his check up every week as he was often out of town. She sent him what she wanted him to have and spent the rest taking care of the house but even more importantly making sure that our church dues were paid.

My sister and I also learned to work early in our lives. At thirteen I was selling papers for the Atlanta Journal Constitution after school. With both mama and daddy working and both of them making decent money plus me and my sister working you'd think that we'd be at least a middle class family. Shoot, my mama was a vice president at Fulton National Bank. But, there was church dues and then there was pastor's rally every year and we spent most of the rest of the year preparing for this major event in our life.

Most churches pay their pastor a salary and have a special appreciation or anniversary day for them each year in which the members show their appreciation by giving gifts or money.

At the FBH church I grew up in the pastor was paid once a year during what was known as "pastor's rally" in late November. Each member was required to give a certain amount from adult down to the youngest child. As I recall all adults eighteen and older were required to give five thousand dollars minimum; teenagers between the ages of sixteen and eighteen one thousand dollars; teenagers between thirteen and sixteen five hundred dollars and everyone twelve and under one hundred dollars, parents responsibility. My mama was a deaconess with ten people under her and thus she was required to give more than any of her members. Usually she had to come up with around seven or eight thousand dollars. So we sold cakes, costume jewelry, candy apples or whatever made a few bucks throughout the year to prepare for this rally in November. We sold barbeque on Saturday nights in front of the liquor store and this was a major money maker.

The deacons and deaconess's, eight groups with eight to twenty members each, not including children would compete against each other on pastor rally night to see which group could out give the other taking turns yelling out amounts between songs. I could hear my mama who was always deacon number seven, "deacon number seven reports, five thousand dollars." And this would continue until all the deacons had reported all the money they had raised. The group that raised the most money was given a big trophy to keep until the next year and praised as the best. We were proud to hear when mama won or even came in second. The children and young adult Sunday school classes would compete in similar manner.

As I write this missive though and look back in retrospect, the FBH church we attended played a major role in my early life development and even in my crime, though yet again, I take full responsibility for the choices that I made and put the blame and fault only on myself. You see the church taught that the greatest sin that a man can commit is that of homosexuality. They taught that to kill homosexuals was to do God a favor. All homosexuals needed to be put to death. Then they had me up in counsel meeting saying that the Spirit had prophesied that I would be a homosexual. Can you see a connection here? Well, maybe this will help: both the victims of my crime were homosexuals, well one was only suspected to be and maybe this suspistion of mine was only a justification to assuage my guilt for the crime.

A psychologist in prison once went so far as to tell me that he felt this church was the sole cause of me committing my crimes and my diagnosis at that time of being bi-polar. He felt that I should appeal my case on the grounds that I did not rationally know what I was doing when I committed my crime as I had been brain washed by the church. He also wanted to report the abuse of the church to law enforcement authorities. But I on the other hand was still too afraid to do any such thing as it seemed that all the church prophesies had come true with the exception of me being homosexual. Throughout my time in prison I guarded myself in the fear that somehow, against my will I would become a homosexual. I had written the church from prison asking their forgiveness and that they pray for me. Of course I never received a response.

"And he said unto him, If now I have found grace in thy sight, then shew me a sign that thou talkest with me." Judges 6:17 (KJV)

After I was sentenced for my crimes I was sent to Georgia's Diagnostic center in Jackson Georgia where they classify new and incoming inmates into the prison system. While there I began to once again get in tune with God. I remembered my experience in Cedartown and the peace that I had felt throughout the arrest and trial process. I was locked in a small cell by myself and was able to read my bible, pray and talk to God without a lot interruption for the next three months.

Prior to my incarceration for these serious offenses I had been sentenced to two years probation for a theft by taking charge and only had a few months left on that sentence when I was given the life plus twenty-two years. While in Jackson I asked God to show me that He was really still with me and that all of this was somehow in His will (If not His perfect will then His permissive will). I asked God to show me that if He chose to that He could release me at any time He chose. That way when He was ready he could and would release me. I was not asking God to release me at that time because I already knew that there was a lesson and a preparation that I needed to go through. I just wanted a sign that He could do so at His will. I had no idea how or what kind of sign He could give me to prove this to me. However, I had totally forgotten about the two years probation I had.

Three days after I prayed and asked God to give me a sign that He could release me anytime he chose to, my name was called over the intercom and I was told to pack my belongings to leave. I was in total disbelief at this and called and asked a guard if in fact they had called my name and for what purpose. Yes my name had been called and yes I was being released.

Once I entered the release area I was told that my two years revoked probation was completed and that I was being released. Oh, my God! My mind was going at a thousand thoughts a minute. "Should I let them release me?" I definitely wanted to go home. But God may be testing me to see if I was going to do the right thing. As I pondered these choices it came to light that a mistake had been made and that I had other sentences to serve. I'm glad that God took that choice out of my hand as I have full confidence that I would have failed that test. But God did not fail! He provided me with an answer to my prayer and proof that He was in control of my destiny. "For I know the thoughts that I think toward you, saith the LORD, thoughts of peace, and not of evil, to give you an expected end" (Jeremiah 29:11, KJV).

Some will argue that we should not tempt or test God like this and support their argument with the quote that Jesus used when the devil tried to get Him to tempt God by jumping off the high mountain: "And Jesus answering said unto him, It is said, Thou shalt not tempt the Lord thy God" (Luke 4:12, Jesus quoting Deut. 6:16, KJV). In response I give two scriptures I've already quoted: "Beloved, believe not every spirit, but try the spirits whether they are of God: because many false prophets are gone out into the world" (1 John 4:1, KJV); "and he said unto him, If now I have found grace in thy sight, then shew me a sign that thou talkest with me" (Judges 6:17, KJV).

I believe God will do more for the new or baby Christian than for a seasoned Christian. Or maybe not so much that He will do more but He will do what is necessary to build the faith of a new convert or struggling Christian to bring them to a state of faith or trusting Him. Regardless, God answered for me and I knew that He was with me.

"And we know that all things work together for good to them that love God, to them who are the called according to his purpose" (Romans 8:28, KJV).

After Diagnostics and classification I was sent to the one prison that I had asked both God and the prison officials not to send me to, Georgia Industrial Institute, aka "ALTO", aka "Lil Reidsville." I'd have rather went to the real Reidsville where all the harden offenders were sent rather than to Alto. Alto was for young offenders usually under the age of twenty with serious and violent crimes. Many if not most had long sentences. It was also the most violent of all the institutions. Alto was on the news regularly for its violence and, while in both the county jail and in Jackson everyone talked about Alto and not wanting to go there. Even the big and bad bullies cringed at the thought of going to Alto, and I was by no means big, bad or bully. In fact I was about five feet ten, one hundred thirty pounds with a smooth hairless face. "The Lord protects the unwary; when I was brought low, he saved me" (Psalm 116:6, NIV).

While on the bus ride from Jackson to Alto I met a young white guy who I made a pack with that we would look out for each other. What I didn't know was that blacks and whites did not socialize in prison and particularly in this prison. White inmates in this prison were nothing more than prey. They were outnumbered probably twenty five to one or more. It is my belief even to this day some forty plus years later that the whites were sent to Alto for the sole purpose of giving the blacks something to keep them calm. What I would later find out is that only the white guys that had given the staff trouble in Jackson or were openly gay was sent to Alto or when they simply didn't have bed space anywhere else. You see, most if not all of the white guys in Alto were homosexual. Not born this way, and not by choice. It was forced on them. They found a big black guy to protect and take care of them as his jailhouse wife or they were passed from one to another.

As the bus pulled up to the prison gate there were numerous inmates on the other side of the gate yelling and screaming at the bus. When we got off the bus we realized that they were picking and choosing "fresh new meat" to be their jailhouse wives with the majority focus on the one white guy on the bus.

After having our heads shaved, and being sprayed with lice shampoo while showering we spoke with the classification inmates. (The head shaving, the showering and lice spraying was all supervised and done by inmates who were suppose to be supervised by a officer). The classification inmates told us what we could and could not have. Anything of value that they wanted and we wouldn't freely give we couldn't have anyway and we had ten days to send it home. Only later we'd see said item on another inmate or in a poker game. We were also assigned our dorm by these inmates and promised a "good dorm" if we had something of value to give.

Several of us, me and the one white guy included were assigned to dorm eleven the kitchen dorm. Everyone in this dorm worked in the kitchen or dining hall.

I could not see or know why I was here and why God had not answered my prayers not to send me here. It would only be later in life that I realize that this was a part of God's plan to educated me and teach me to trust Him. It was here that I learned that God does not hate anyone; not even homosexuals even though He doesn't condone their deeds. We should not judge another person's actions as we do not know what circumstance brought that person to that choice or what was or is in that persons heart.

"Yea, though I walk through the valley of the shadow of death, I will fear no evil: for thou art with me; thy rod and thy staff they comfort me." Psalms 23:4 (KJV)

The twenty third psalms is one of the constant testimonies of God in my life and particularly this fourth verse.

On my second day in Alto I went "through the valley of the shadow of death" and slept through it. That first night there after lights out the white guy had been gang raped. He told no one, not the guards or even me. On the second night while I slept he got his revenge.

I woke the next morning and noticed that a number of the beds were empty including both the beds on either side of me and the top bunk bed I was sleeping under. During the wee hours of the night and early morning I was told the white guy had taped "shanks" (homemade knifes) to both his hand and went up and down the dorm stabbing black guys, always making sure he skipped over me before he was finally stopped. You talk about peace in the midst of a storm! The psalmist best describe it in Psalms 3:5, "I laid me down and slept; I awaked; for the LORD sustained me."

As I reflect back over my life I think of the many, many, times I have walked, ran or even slept "through the valley of the shadow of death." When I was arrested the police came to the house with a whole swat team ready to kill, as they said during my trial that they had heard that I wouldn't be taken alive. While incarcerated I recall an officer telling me that I wouldn't live the week out. I called my Christian mentor and prayer partner, Minister Marks, and that night we prayed for God's protection over the phone. The next day on the way to work that same officer had a wreck and was decapitated. Not that this is anything to boast about but it is a demonstration of God hearing the prayers of the saints and protecting His people.

There are numerous other occasions that I can tell of God's walking me "through the valley of the shadow of death" while I was in prison and since I've been out. Suffice it to say that I witnessed a number of people killed, raped, beat, or even commit suicide while I was in prison yet I can honestly say that God protected me for twenty six plus years from any of this happening to me.

My own roommate and best friend at one time got mad at God because he was denied parole; changed his religious beliefs, which means he was never really rooted in Christ in the first place, raped the librarian at the prison, cut her up with a razor, and then killed himself.

Prison is a nasty place. Though a lot has changed over the years for the better in prison it still is a nasty place.

"Trust in the LORD with all thine heart; and lean not unto thine own understanding" (Proverbs 3:5, KJV).

Just as the children of Israel often forgot the red sea crossing, the water from a rock, manna from heaven and the many other miracles God had done in their presence so I once again did the same. As I did earlier when I first got to the county jail I forgot all God had already done for me. I felt that "I" had to do something to improve my situation. Instead of trusting God I started trusting my own schemes. I had two thoughts in my head: one I had to protect myself and two, if my brothers had escaped so could I. It was either escape or spend the rest of my life in this prison and if I escaped there would be no need for me to have to worry about protecting myself from anyone. So I put together a plan and briefly escaped from the prison. From the prison itself but I didn't get too far before howling dogs and prison guards caught up to me, beat the crap out of me, and took me back and put me in the hole. (The hole was isolation, alone in a dark small cell with loss of mail, phone and visitation privileges and no access to television or radio). Before the courts, sometime in the early nineties, ruled it cruel and unusual punishment all they fed you in the hole was what we called mush. Mush consisted of all the meals the rest of the inmate population had during the week, grinded up together into a sort of loaf. You had eggs, chicken, grits, oatmeal, cereal, pork chops, collards, black-eyed peas, green bean and a lot more from the previous week mashed together and given to you in one meal a day with a cup of warm water. You went in the hole weighing one hundred sixty pounds and came out weighing one hundred and thirty five pounds or less depending on how long you stayed in.

I was supposed to have stayed there for a minimum of six months but got real sick after about six weeks and had to be transported to the "free world hospital," which gave me a future idea about how I could escape.

When I was taken back to the prison I was placed once again in dorm eleven. I wasn't back long before I found myself back in the hole. As I lay on my bunk I noticed this one guy kept staring at me. Seemed every time I looked up he was staring at me. God protecting me "through the valley of the shadow of death" was the farthest thing from my mind. I had to do something to protect myself! I didn't know how to make a shank and even if I did I didn't have anything to make one of. About three that morning I took a mop ringer and went to work on dudes head. Back to the hole I went.

The next day I was sent to see the mental health director and a psychologist. When asked why I had attacked the other inmate I told them because he kept staring at me; "No he hadn't said anything to me" and "no he hadn't done anything to me other than staring at me." It was decided that I had a mental health issue. I was moved to my own personal room in the mental health ward. I had no complaint. Over here if I didn't want to go to the cafeteria to eat they brought my food to me.

PART THREE
PLEASE BE PATIENT WITH ME

"Whom shall he teach knowledge? and whom shall he make to understand doctrine? them that are weaned from the milk, and drawn from the breasts. For precept must be upon precept, precept upon precept; line upon line, line upon line; here a little, and there a little"(Isaiah 28:9-10, KJV)

    I had dropped out of school after the ninth grade but I was always considered "book smart." While in school I was an "A" student for the most part. I was given the choice in Alto of going to school or returning to work back in the kitchen or out cutting grass. I chose school and within two weeks I had taken and passed the GED test scoring amongst the highest percentile scores in the state. For the next couple of weeks I used my newly labeled mental health status to avoid working any details except cleaning the building I was staying in.

Finally I was approached by one of the counselors about going to college. I informed him that college was for white folks, which of course is what I had always been told. When I was in school we all concentrated on getting out of school and going to work or joining the military. The counselor told me that this was a stereotype that I needed to help break. He convinced me that black people were just as smart as whites. (This was a white counselor).

What was going on with me, in my life? Not only was I going to college, the only black there at that time, but I was intently studying the bible and felt drawn and compelled to push harder in these studies. I felt as if I was the only one in this whole prison system that was actually trying to get right with God. It was as if none of the other inmates knew or cared anything about God. I was being forced to grow up mentally and spiritually.

"Go down to the potter's house, and there I will give you my message." So I went down to the potter's house, and I saw him working at the wheel. But the pot he was shaping from the clay was marred in his hands; so the potter formed it into another pot, shaping it as seemed best to him" (Jeremiah 18:1-4, NIV)

Though I didn't realize it at that time I was being "transformed by the renewing of my mind" (Romans 12:2), I was on the "potter's wheel."

"Judge not, that ye be not judged. For with what judgment ye judge, ye shall be judged: and with what measure ye mete, it shall be measured to you again. And why beholdest thou the mote that is in thy brother's eye, but considerest not the beam that is in thine own eye?" (Matt. 7:1-3, KJV)

Much was going on during this time of study. I found myself the inmate counselor in the mental health dorm. The other inmates seemed to have found a trust in me wherein they revealed their innermost thoughts, secrets and crimes. I came to find that the majority of the people in mental health were here for sexual abuse cases, pedophiles in particular, or murder. But hearing their stories caused me to pity them instead of the anger or hate I would have expected.

They all wanted to know what I thought of their crimes and more importantly if they were condemned to hell. I soon became known as the "story teller" as I would answer their questions by telling them one of the stories out of the bible, in a way that they could understand and comparing their situations to those of the people in the bible. These people were from all walks of life, raised Muslim, Catholic, Christian, even some Indian faiths and so called atheist. Yet, they all seem to want to know if their soul was condemned to hell.

One of the first clear messages that God gave to me in dealing with these inmates was that I was no better than they. God brought to my attention that not only had I killed one person but two. I tried to justify this with God by telling Him that neither one of my victims was a child nor had I sexually abused any one. God's reply to me was to ask me if the victims of my crime had parents? Well, yes they did. Then they were somebody's child and thus I had indeed taken the life of a child. If nothing else they were His children.

"So when they continued asking him, he lifted up himself, and said unto them, He that is without sin among you, let him first cast a stone at her" (John 8:7, KJV).

Not only have the inmates in prison been judged and found guilty by a court of law, by their families, and even by themselves but by the whole world in general. Even the churches and the Christian community have no mercy or compassion on those who have been convicted of crimes. "The Lord is gracious and righteous; our God is full of compassion" (Psalm 116:5, NIV).

But the finding of guilt is not the issue, but the lack of forgiveness. We accept and expect the blood of Jesus to wash our sins away but we separate our sins from those who are in prison and feel that we have no need to forgive them nor do we expect "our" God to do so.

And when ye stand praying, forgive, if ye have ought against any: that your Father also which is in heaven may forgive you your trespasses. But if ye do not forgive, neither will your Father which is in heaven forgive your trespasses" (Mark 11:25-26, KJV).

"But God has chosen the foolish things of the world to put to shame the wise, and God has chosen the weak things of the world to put to shame the things which are mighty; and the base things of the world and the things which are despised God has chosen..." 1 Corinthians 1:27-28 (KJV)

Even though I was ministering to the inmates in the mental health unit I didn't feel or think of it in terms of me ministering to anybody. It seemed to be coming naturally to me, just something I was doing. I didn't feel that I was qualified to be ministering to folks about God. Daily I was convincing others that God would forgive them and helping them to feel better about themselves while on the other hand I didn't feel that this same message of God's forgiveness applied to me.

I was praying daily and reading the bible daily. Teaching the bible to others through the biblical stories I was telling. God was revealing things to me, giving me the words and inspiration for the others and I was actually talking to God on a daily basis, but still.... When it came to me personally.... I had a relationship with God and on a subconscious level I knew, but consciously I was not thinking of it in this way.

Was I saved? Again I didn't think in terms of being saved or not saved. I believed that I had gotten saved prior to my incarceration on the living floor in Cedartown Georgia. Saved to me at that time simply meant that I would not die and go to hell. But I still smoked cigarettes; loved to play poker many evening (not for fun).

It would only be later as I grew from a babe in Christ that I would learn about the "process" of sanctification and that "being saved" was a livelong endeavor. Listening to the radio and TV ministries and preachers helped a great deal in my growth and learning experience. (Kenneth Hagan, Dr. Paul Walker and Charles Stanley and T.D. Jakes were among the few who helped me to grow in my Christian walk).

I had to realize as I was telling others about how God chose those who didn't appear to be qualified, to lift them up and convince them of their place in God's plan, that this also included me. (Murdering and stuttering Moses, murdering adulterer King David, Young and innocent Jeremiah, brash and deserting Peter, Saint persecutor Paul). There is only one person, one human being that has ever been born without sin and in perfection. Jesus Christ, Lord of Lord and King of Kings, Son of the Living God!

Righteous comes by and through Jesus. "God made him who had no sin to be sin for us, so that in him we might become the righteousness of God." 2 Corinthians 5:21 (NIV)

"For all have sinned, and come short of the glory of God; Being justified freely by his grace through the redemption that is in Christ Jesus:" Romans 3:23-24 (KJV)

Many people that I minister to today and work with, when they hear my testimony say "I just can't believe that you been to prison" or "I can't believe that you have done all of those things.

We as a society seem to judge people by their appearance or by how much they have or don't have; where they live, the color of their skin or any other outward appearing displays. Fortunately, God judges by faith and character, not appearances. And because only God can see our inside condition, our heart, only He can accurately judge us. Many people allow me into their homes, businesses without the slightest notion that I am a two time convicted murderer. And even after they find out, because of the grace and mercy God has shown me and because of the way I carry myself along with the testimony I give, they still accept me.

There was a young lady on my job that I was ministering to quite often. She trusted me more than she trusted her parents. She was Catholic and revealed her innermost thoughts and secrets to me seeking my advice on how to handle many of life's situations that she was going through. But she use to always make the statement that in her opinion God should never forgive a murderer as they are the worst people along with pedophiles in the whole world. She never knew about my crimes.

I mentioned earlier the victims of my crime were homosexuals and I thought, and was taught that I was doing God a favor. Here recently, (this was in 2008) I passed by a prominent church in Atlanta where people were standing outside with signs stating that "God hates homosexuals"; and "queers die"; "Aids is God's curse on gays and blessing to the rest of society."

This is what the Apostle Paul was doing to the Christian's before his conversion, thinking that he was doing God a favor.

"And I thank Christ Jesus our Lord, who hath enabled me, for that he counted me faithful, putting me into the ministry; who was before a blasphemer, and a persecutor, and injurious: but I obtained mercy, because I did *it* ignorantly in unbelief. And the grace of our Lord was exceeding abundant with faith and love which is in Christ Jesus. This *is* a faithful saying, and worthy of all acceptation, that Christ Jesus came into the world to save sinners; of whom I am chief. Howbeit for this cause I obtained mercy, that in me first Jesus Christ might shew forth all longsuffering, for a pattern to them which should hereafter believe on him to life everlasting." 1 Timothy 1:12-16 (KJV)

Due to the overcrowding problems in the prison the inmates in the mental health units had to be doubled up two to a room. For the next year or so I became best friends with my roommate. This guy came to the prison when he was fourteen years old with a life sentence for the rape and murder of his eight year old niece. He had several mental health diagnoses.

Maybe I'm naïve or maybe a bit slow, but it took me over a year of being this guy's roommate before I realized he was a homosexual. He was actually doing his thing with other guys when I went to college every night or while I was out playing poker. I was first told this while playing poker one night and of course I didn't believe it. I discovered it was true when I came back from college early one night because the instructor didn't show up.

I ended up back in the hole. Even though I had been in a number of altercations by this time, this was the first time I choked a person out. I thought I had killed again. This guy eventually became my best friend and a true ambassador for Christ himself.

"A good reputation and respect are worth much more than silver and gold." Prov. 22:1 (CEV)

There was a lot that went on during the nearly ten years I stayed in Alto. I joined the boxing and weightlifting teams and became the states lightweight boxing champion and placed second or third every year in the states power lifting competitions in my weight division. In November every year all the institutions gathered together at Jackson Diagnostic Center to compete in the Prison Olympics: In competitions ranging from chess, checkers and back gammon to basketball, softball, boxing, weightlifting and much more.

I earned ninety plus hours in college while at Alto, as we were only allowed to enroll in one or two classes per quarter. I was less than fifteen hours away from graduation when I was transferred in early nineteen-ninety.

There was another escape attempt that didn't even get as far as the first one: the entire mental health dorm I was in had to be quarantined. I was the only inmate in the dorm of about a hundred folks who didn't catch gonorrhea, a sexually transmitted disease: There were deaths, suicides and homicides, inside the prison and the dorm itself; rapes and assaults were rampant, even armed robberies. Alto lived up to its name during that time as the most violent institution in the state and one of the most violent in the country.

Through it all I continued to be "the story teller", continued to pray and read my bible, and had earned the trust of nearly the entire prison population and staff. Inmates all over the prison, not just mental health, requested my presence and prayers when they were in crisis, when there was sickness and death in their families; when the girlfriends or wives sent "Dear John" letters. In many of the situations God seem to answer my prayers for people and their families which in essence caused more people to come to me. The staff also began to ask for my prayers and advice, which is why I had to be transferred. It was thought amongst the authorities that, as an inmate myself, I had gained too much power in this institution.

I still had my main two vices: smoking and gambling and even went through a phase of a few months where I sold drugs. So I know that it was not all my own goodness that carried me but the mercy and grace of God as well as the prayers of the saints, my grandmother, mother and others who were constantly in prayer for me.

"The Lord is not slow in keeping his promise, as some understand slowness. Instead he is patient with you, not wanting anyone to perish, but everyone to come to repentance." 2 Peter 3:9 (NIV)

Grace means to get something that you do not deserve; unmerited favor. Mercy means that you do not get a punishment that you do deserve; compassion and forbearance. God is abundant in grace and mercy and I know that God had a plan for my life.

"Let us therefore come boldly unto the throne of grace that we may obtain mercy, and find grace to help in time of need." Hebrews 4:16 (KJV)

PART FOUR
ANGELS

"See, I am sending an angel ahead of you to guard you along the way and to bring you to the place I have prepared." Exodus 23:20 (NIV)

Being in Alto from nineteen-eighty two until nineteen ninety-three, not only had institutionalization taken place in my life but also institutionalization for the place Alto itself. I was transferred to Frank Scott Correctional Institute in Milledgeville Georgia.

After only twenty days in this new institution I ended up first in the hospital in a coma for three weeks from an overdose suicide attempt. In actuality it was the second time I had attempted suicide. I was told had I been found fifteen minutes later I would have succeeded. I was sent from the hospital to the prison mental health crisis unit. (I had come off the mental health case load well before I left Alto, but was assigned a detail working with the mental health unit as an inmate counselor).

It was here in this mental health crisis unit that I met the mental health director, Ms. Simmons, and through her my life started to change forever for the better. I had vowed to her during our first meeting at the hospital that once I was returned to the institution I would try again to commit suicide and that I would continue to try until I succeeded. She asked me to give her ninety days to change my mind and I agreed, not really intending to. God used this director to convince me that I had cause to live.

To this day I have no idea how Ms. Simmons arraigned some of the things she did. As I stated earlier, when I was arrested my girlfriend was pregnant. The last time I had heard from her was when my son was born in March of nineteen-eighty three and she sent me pictures of him.

Within a week after I left the crisis unit I was sitting in the visitation room with my nine year old son and my now ex girlfriend. The following week my mother, father, sister and other family members visited and were allowed to bring dinner in with them. I was convinced that suicide was not so much a cowardly act as many argue, because I didn't care anything about being called a coward, but it was a selfish act that not only would hurt me but also those that I loved and who loved me. The mental health director, being a Christian herself, also talked of how much it would hurt God and interrupt His plans for my life.

I soon begin to run into many different mental health and prison officials who had a relationship with God and a genuine concern for the inmates. These were angel sent from God.

Over the next year at this institution I begin yet again to build a reputation as "the story teller" and a trusted person among the inmates and the staff. It was this trust in me by another inmate that caused me to have to be transferred yet again.

"Trust in the Lord with all thine heart; and lean not unto thine own understanding. In all thy ways acknowledge him, and he shall direct thy paths." Proverbs 3:5-6 (KJV)

As I sat in the mental health director's office listening, she told me I had to be transferred again for my own protection; a part of me began to sink. But, unlike the last time I was transferred there was something inside of me that held me up this time. I would later come to realize that as Christians, growing Christians, we go through test. Failing a test will cause you to have to re-take that test again. Was I going to fail this test yet again and have to repeat it? Thanks to Almighty God and His forever grace, for the people He had sent into my life and the knowledge I had acquired…!

So why did I have to be transferred again? I had met another inmate who, once again, wanted my opinion as to his chances of making it into heaven or if he was doomed to hell for the things he had done in his life. So begin a week long confessional. I personally couldn't believe all the things this inmate claimed to have done. He was serving a life sentence for murder. But he claimed that he had murdered and raped at least eight others and had never been suspected for them. He gave me details of the murders and the rapes of these eight people, some of them children. He even told me where he had disposed of the bodies, what they were wearing, how he met them and all sort of other details. I didn't believe any of it.

I informed him that if any of this was true that he had to first confess his sins to God and that there was hope for him even if this was true. As long as he had breath in his body there was the opportunity to seek and receive forgiveness. Didn't one of the men on the cross with Jesus in his final hour seek forgiveness and was forgiven? Luke 23:40-43. He then had to confess his crimes to man and tell the parents and family of those missing where they were so that they could have closure and then he had to seek their forgiveness. If they chose not to forgive him then it was they who must answer to God not him.

As the next couple of weeks passed my mind kept coming back to these confessions and I kept putting them aside as a tale of somebody who wanted to feel or be important. During my next monthly counseling session with the mental health director I showed her my notes from my conversations with this inmate and asked what she thought. She didn't believe any of it either. But because she felt it was bothering me enough for me to write it all down, and because there was so much detail, she suggested that I write the District Attorney in the county where all this was supposed to have happened sending them some of the details I had gotten from this inmate. The worst that could happen is they throw my letter in the trash as non-sense. So I wrote.

Three days later I was called to the warden's office where I was taken into a room where the windows had been covered in black plastic trash bags. The first thing I was told was that they had found a body in the exact place I wrote it would be. The name of the person had been reported missing many years ago.

After establishing the fact that I had been in prison for a decade, some of the missing persons and murders had happened while I was in prison, and that prior to my incarceration I had never before been in their city, they wanted to know what all this inmate had told me; they wanted to see my notes.

Within the next few days more bodies were found. I never found out exactly how many. The inmate was taken back to the county jail where he plead guilty to the crimes and received several more life sentences and, live on TV asked for forgiveness from the victim's families and God.

Somehow my name was leaked to the media and I had to be transferred for my own protection. This time I was asked if there was any other institution I preferred to go to. My first choice was to the institution where my brothers were but I was told that another institution, Phillips State Prison, was just opening closer to my home city of Atlanta and I would be one of the first inmates there. It would be good because there weren't many other inmates there and I could get visits regularly. I was transferred to Phillips, alone, in the middle of the day by the GBI and put in a dorm by myself.

> *"Keep on loving one another as brothers and sisters. Do not forget to show hospitality to strangers, for by so doing some people have shown hospitality to angels without knowing it. Continue to remember those in prison as if you were together with them in prison, and those who are mistreated as if you yourselves were suffering." Hebrews 13:1-3 (NIV)*

Angels! I truly believe that there are human angels. I believe that at times in our lives, if we allow God to use us that we all will be an angel to someone else, to help them through some of life's hardships. Angels are super natural beings at God's command. Sometimes in life there are situations that arise in a person's life that require only "super natural" gifts to overcome. The thing is that many times the person-angel that is helping does not see themselves as an angel nor their help as super natural. But if that help in anyway turned a person's life around and more importantly brought a soul to the knowledge of and a relationship with God then it was indeed, in my opinion, the doings of an angel doing a super-natural deed.

Many Christian churches' today believe that the Pastor of the church is the "Angel" God has appointed over that house. In Genesis 18:2 we read of men-angels visiting the patriot Abraham.

(Angels who came in the form of man). But just as there are angels that come in human form there are humans that come with the mission of an angel.

Mike and Jenny. Angels. I met Mike and Jenny in 1998 and God used these two people to help restore my faith in humanity after going through a very painful ordeal.

I had been assaulted by a prison staff member and my family had hired a law firm to represent me in litigation against this staff person. Mike was an attorney with this law firm though not the one directly working my case. Mike told me at that time that he wanted to meet me because of the legal work I had already done pertaining to this litigation prior to my family hiring a lawyer. He told me the legal work I had done was equal to that of a third year law student.

I don't believe there are "coincident" when it comes to the children of God. Meeting Mike had nothing to do with this litigation. Mike and Jenny were willing vessels of God. They looked beyond my faults; beyond my race; beyond my mental and emotional condition; they looked beyond the crimes I had been convicted of. Mike and Jenny saw into my soul and realized that I was a desperate person looking to please God and to do what was right. As the saying go "they looked beyond my faults and saw my need."

From then, nineteen-ninety eight until now Mike and Jenny have been my family. They have guided and supported me in every aspect of my life. I can't begin to tell all that this family has meant to me and done for me.

When my mother and father's health begin to fail and they couldn't come and visit much, Mike was there and even brought Jenny on occasion; when my family could no longer afford to send me the twenty dollars a month they were sending Mike and Jenny more than took up the slack.

People can't understand why a person needs any money while in prison. The argument is that the state (tax payers) pays for everything. In Georgia's prison whenever you get sick, tooth ache, injured in any way, allergy's, cold, flu or whatever if you have to see a doctor you are charged five dollars; If you want to take pictures to send to your kids, five dollars. More than any of this if you didn't want to go to bed hungry or sick every night you needed funds to buy food with.

The next argument will be that five dollars isn't anything to pay to go to the doctor. In Georgia's prisons the inmates are not paid for working. Five dollars is a great deal to a sick person that doesn't have five dollars; many of nights the food served by the prison and cooked by inmates would itself make you sick. I recall one incident where the prisons were serving some donated pig's feet. Nearly the whole institution was vomiting and had diarrhea that night and the next morning. In another incident an inmate working in the kitchen had put some kind of detergent in the spaghetti sauce. Again nearly the whole institution was in pain vomiting with bloody stools. Incidents with the food like this occurred on a fairly regular basis. The safest bet was to purchase your own food from the inmate commissary.

It wasn't just the money Mike and Jenny sent but they made sure that I had the basic necessities such as underwear, tooth brush, soap, pajamas, wash rags and towels, tennis shoes. They sent me a package every Christmas and on my birthday which they never forgot. The letters, the cards and the pictures was a way of including me in their family outings and vacations by giving me all the details with pictures. I got to cry and pray with them during the hard times and illnesses they and their family went through; when Lester, their cat was eaten by a coyote; when Jenny had their first child. Though I was not there physically I was still there with them for all of this. When my mother or father was sick or in need Mike was there.

When I got home from prison Mike took me under his wing even more. He bought me my first clothe and, without making me feel inadequate or stupid, though I was completely lost, he helped me to pick out the proper things to wear and paid for everything while at the same time putting money in my pocket every week until I found a job.

One year during my second stint in Alto in 2003 Mike sent money to nearly every inmate in the Mental Health Unit for Christmas. When I was down Mike and Jenny were there with a word of encouragement. I could write a whole book on just Mike and Jenny and what they meant to and did for me and the entire mental health units at every institution I went to.

"Go therefore and make disciples of all nations, baptizing them in the name of the Father and of the Son and of the Holy Spirit, teaching them to observe all that I have commanded you." Matthew 28:19-20 (NIV)

      I met Mike and Jenny in 1998 while I was in Valdosta State prison. But before Valdosta was Phillips. When I left Frank Scott in 1991, years before I met Mike and Jenny, God sent another angel into my life; Ozie. Each person in your life is there for a reason. As I stated earlier I do not believe in co-incident or accident. I believe in divine providence. "For those God foreknew he also predestined to be conformed to the image of his Son, that he might be the firstborn among many brothers and sisters." Romans 8:29 (NIV)

I didn't know how to word Ozie's purpose in my life for many years until after I got out of prison and he told me what God had told him his purpose was. Christians often talk about evangelism and bringing people to God. Bro. Ozie's job with me and others that he ministered to goes beyond the task of just bringing people to God. Discipleship. Making people lifetime disciples of Jesus Christ is the duty of all Christian and Christ commanded this himself. Matthew 28:19-20.

During His three years of ministry Jesus' job persisted of making disciples out of His followers not just Christians. Jesus said, "If you hold to my teaching, you are really my disciples." John 8:31 (NIV) Discipleship is a lifelong commitment.

I met Ozie through a prison Christian mentoring program. Ozie had volunteered to mentor an inmate that had no family. The mentors were to be family for those who had none, visiting them, sending them the necessities they needed as well, talking to them on the phone and writing letter to them while at the same time ministering the word to them. Helping to prepare these inmates for life after prison and maintaining a relationship with God when released. I was a part of the mentoring group bible study but was not suppose to have a personal mentor because I had family and I also had life without parole and was not suppose to ever get out of prison.

Ozie's first inmate he was assigned to mentor didn't want him as a mentor because this guy was looking for a female mentor that he could have a relationship with. All he wanted Ozie to do was to hook him up with some "ladies" and possibly send him some money. I think Ozie tried another inmate who had a similar issue and Ozie told me later that he was about to quit the program when he decided that he would try one more inmate. While the institution went through the filtering process of trying to find an eligible inmate that was considered a match with Ozie they asked if I would stand in allowing Ozie to mentor me for awhile. Providence! God's divine intervention.

Ozie became my very best friend in the world and still is now some twenty plus years later. The first words out of Brother Ozie's mouth to me during our first visit were "I'm going to be real with you and you need to be real with me or we're not going to get anywhere." Brother Ozie was bringing this great big, almost table sized, Bible to the visitation room every week. For the next twenty years we discussed every merit of life that came up in our lives and what God had to say on the issue. Every issue, from the smallest to the biggest that came up we discussed in the light of what God wants us to do.

With the exception of maybe my mother, Ozie, as far as people I know, had the closest relationship with God of anybody I ever met. Ozie has prayed me through when I saw no way through; I've cried on his shoulder a many of time and whenever I needed anything Ozie was there. I would call Ozie and try to explain that I needed this or that for this reason or another and before I could get the reasons out of my mouth he'd tell me it didn't matter what you need it for you are a brother in Christ and if I got it to give you can have it.

Ozie also became very close with my mother, bringing her to visit me regularly when she could no longer drive; visiting her when she went into the hospital; taking her out on her birthday and helping her pay her bills. When my father passed and me and my brother couldn't attend the funeral Ozie was there with my mother. When I paroled from prison I paroled to Ozie's house; Ozie picked me up from the prison when I was released.

Years before I was paroled my mother went to see the Governor about granting me a parole and was told that I would never leave prison. When I read the letter it started to depress me a bit, though not much, because I wasn't expecting to get out anyway. Ozie's words to me were "if you will take care of God's business he'll take care of yours." Ozie taught me to focus on pleasing God and working to improve my personal relationship with God while at the same time witnessing to others about and for God.

For many years I considered myself a "closet Christian." By this I mean that I witnessed only to people one on one or in small groups, never contributing in bible class or participating in worship services and only when others approached me. "Get out of your comfort zone." This was Ozie's message to me. I soon joined the prison choir, and became head of a program called inmates participation where we prayed for and witnessed to others both inside of and outside the prison walls. I soon found myself "speaking" to youth groups and being allowed to go out to speak at churches. Speaking turned into teaching which turned into preaching without me even realizing what was happening. Then I was approached by a pastor and told that the Lord had instructed him to ordain me for a future work for God. I became an ordain minister of the gospel though I felt I had already been ordained by God.

I had not thought about or mentioned getting out of prison for a long while and had even told my mother not to spend any more money or time trying to get me out of prison as this is where God intended me to be. Some years later, in early 2007 another minister, Brother Darryl, came to me after a service and told me that God had come to him and told him that I would be released from prison that year. But he said I had to start claiming and proclaiming this so that God could get the glory. I was very hesitant about this and it was only after listening to Brother Darryl preach several other sermons on faith that the Holy spirit gave me the confidence and faith to start making these proclamations. I became loud and clear to everyone that God was about to release me from prison. The warden was so worried about me making these claims, and when he or no one could dissuade me from them, he had me put back in mental health.

"... do not forsake your mother's teaching." Proverbs 1:8 (NIV)

My mother, Gwendolyn Dillard, drilled the bible into my head. From my earliest memories to her death I cannot remember a conversation with my mother that did not have something to do with the Bible, God, salvation and most importantly Jesus Christ. I don't think there were many people who did know or speak to my mother that she did not at one time or another witness to. My mother stood by my side from beginning to end. My crimes didn't affect her love for me.

As I watched and witnessed many other inmates being raped, brutalized and killed in prison, I believe it was the prayers of my mother that protected me from this. "The prayer of a righteous person is powerful and effective." James 5:16 (NIV) She visited both my brothers and me as often as she could. She was constantly going trying to get help to get us out of prison. We could not call or get a visit from mama without getting a sermon from her about what God was doing or going to do in our lives. She constantly reminded us that God had a plan for our lives.

My mama was a kind and generous person. She took whole families of strangers into her house and when we, being my sister and I, tried to tell mama she needed to learn to tell people no her reply was, "if someone ask me for something and I give it to them, and that person is taking advantage of me, then they will be accountable to God for that; but on the other hand if that person asks and I refuse to give it and they needed it, then I will be accountable to God.

My mother told people that God had promised her that she would not see death until she saw all of her boys free from prison. God was faithful to this word to my mother. All praise honor and worship to Almighty God for this woman of God!

PART FIVE
"...BUT I DON'T BELIEVE HE BROUGHT ME THIS FAR TO LEAVE ME"

"For I am already being poured out as a drink offering, and the time of my departure has come. I have fought the good fight, I have finished the course, I have kept the faith…" 2 Timothy 4:6-7 (NIV)

       In July two-thousand seven I received a letter from the state parole board stating that after reconsidering my status they had decided to grant me parole on September seventeenth; only two months away. Even though I had been proclaiming this nearly all year I still couldn't believe it. The warden, my counselor and no one else could believe it either; except for Brother Darryl, Brother Ozie and my jubilant mother. Two years earlier my brother Jeffery had been granted parole after serving over thirty years. My brother Wayne had been given a medical reprieve back in ninety-one and had passed away from AIDS in ninety-three. I was the last one left. Mama's prayer was about to be answered.

There were many people from the warden down to my counselor telling me that it was not all about "God" releasing me but also because of my attitude and growth since I had been in prison. But I knew better; you see my attitude and growth was all a result of the grace and mercy of God. "And those he predestined, he also called; those he called, he also justified; those he justified, he also glorified." Romans 8:30 (NIV). "No one can come to me unless the Father who sent me draws them, and I will raise them up at the last day." John 6:44 (NIV)

When I made the announcement at that Friday night inmates service that I was being released it was a bitter sweet moment. Many of the inmates and staff were sad to hear I was leaving while at the same time it encouraged many others that if God would answer my prayers and grant me this miracle then He could do the same thing for them. That Friday night's inmate participation services was a room full of convicted murderers, rapist, and gang members and harden correction officers crying and giving God praise.

"Remember the wonders he has done, his miracles, and the judgments he pronounced." 1 Chronicles 16:12 (NIV)

Over these twenty six years much had happened that I haven't written about. I stopped gambling back when I arrived in Frank Scott. I was sent back to Alto in two thousand where I meet Mr. Helton the mental health director, and a man who fought hard to get me a parole date; Brother Ozie sponsored Christian cookouts for the inmates there and after I settled my lawsuit against the state prison system for the assault on me by a staff member, for Christmas that year I sent every inmate in one of the mental health dorms fifty to a hundred dollars each. It was over a hundred inmates in all.

In May two thousand four I quit smoking finally. I had been told by a Christian friend of mine that even though he didn't believe that smoking would put me in hell that it sure made me smell like hell and, as a minister of the Gospel I didn't look good smoking. After praying about it for what seemed like the thousandth time, I told God that I enjoyed smoking and that I couldn't and didn't want to quit. I told God that if He wanted me to quit that He would have to take the desire from me miraculously and that I was not going to try to quit on my own again. Exactly seven days later, on a Friday, I woke up and just didn't want to smoke anymore. I haven't smoked a cigarette since. To God be the glory! I had tried to keep my smoking hid from Brother Ozie but he later told me that he knew all along that I was smoking and he knew when I stopped.

As I think about many of the people I knew over the years I realize that not all of them were real with God. I think about Pharaoh in Egypt and how he kept hardening his heart against God. I realized that people who do this is and has never been real with God in the first place. "Therefore God has mercy on whom he wants to have mercy, and he hardens whom he wants to harden." Romans 9:18 (NIV). This is what happened to my friend Harold.

"The seed falling on rocky ground refers to someone who hears the word and at once receives it with joy. But since they have no root, they last only a short time. When trouble or persecution comes because of the word, they quickly fall away." Matthew 13:20-21 (NIV)

I mentioned my roommate and best friend at Phillips, Harold, earlier. Harold and I were "coming out" enthusiastic Christians at Phillips. We attended all the worship services, Bible studies and choir practices; we held a Bible study on the dorm we were in and every Friday we held a intercessory prayer for inmates and staff who presented issues they needed or wanted prayed for. With me playing the bass and Harold on the drums we even wrote a gospel song "Most Holy God." It was here at Phillips that the state certified me and Harold as the first two inmates in the state prison system as certified law library clerks and begin sending us around the state to other institutions to work the law libraries and assist other inmates in legal matters ranging from divorce, child custody and legitimating to appeals and law suits. This went on until other inmates in the state were trained and each institution had at least two trained law library clerks.

It was also here at Phillips that Harold used a box cutter to assault the librarian and then went on to commit suicide. Harold went off because he was denied parole. His entire Christian faith and actions were based on the premise of God releasing him from prison when he came up for parole. I never thought about this the many times he testified that he "knew" without a doubt that God was going to release him when he came up for parole. I had faith that God had somehow revealed this to him and was going to perform it. Immediately after the parole denial Harold became a Muslim, showing as much devotion to it as he had being a Christian. A few months after his Islamic conversion came the assault and suicide.

Harold was already serving a life sentence for killing his girlfriend. Prior to our Christian campaign beginning Harold used to always talk bad about and down to women. He even talked about killing his own mother and sister when they didn't send him money or do other things he wanted them to do. Only when we got into the Bible did he cease this talk. I think that even though Harold was not fully grounded in the word, it still had an effect on his life. "For the word of God is alive and active. Sharper than any double-edged sword, it penetrates even to dividing soul and spirit, joints and marrow; it judges the thoughts and attitudes of the heart." Hebrews 4:12 (NIV) When he was assigned to the law library I personally went and talked to the deputy warden about my fear of him working with a female without any security around. My warnings were dismissed as unfounded. Harold and the librarian began a personal and sexual relationship and she too dismissed my fears as unmerited. When the prison system stopped all smoking in the system this librarian would bring case upon case of cigarettes for me and Harold to sell: five dollars for one cigarette and twenty five for a pack.

Most of society thinks that anyone who professes to follow or have found Jesus in prison does so only for some ulterior motive as Harold did. "Jesus answered them, "It is not the healthy who need a doctor, but the sick. I have not come to call the righteous, but sinners to repentance." Luke 5:31-32 (NIV) Paul was in prison for years, and the argument that he wasn't guilty of the crimes charged doesn't work to separate him from the rest of us who have been in prison and who still serve and honor God after our release. He was guilty of persecuting the saints. Instead of always condemning, the church needs to be leading these people towards converting and making disciples of those in prison. Just as there are many that pretend to follow Christ for various different reason in prison there are also the few that are true to their following of Christ.

"Still other seed fell on good soil. It came up, grew and produced a crop, some multiplying thirty, some sixty, some a hundred times." Mark 4:8 (NIV)

As many pretentious Christians as there are in prison there are also those that are real. Behind the walls of the prison is just a mini version of the outside world in nearly every aspect of life. There are relationships both hetero and homo; deaths, funeral memorials, marriages (men marrying their fiancée's from the free world) and just as in the free world there are real and fake Christians. I was once told that you will only find Christian hypocrites in church. But we still do not classify or stereotype everyone in the church or even in the streets that profess to be a

Christian as hypocrites. Neither are all the professing Christians in prison hypocrites. But for the grace of God many of those pointing the fingers would have, could have, or should have been in prison.

Kevin was in prison for child molestation. To my understanding he had been in for fifteen years on a twenty year sentence. He had sex with a fifteen year old girl. I met Kevin during the final five years of my incarceration at Rutledge State Prison in Columbus GA. Soon after Bro. Ozie had told me I needed to "get out of my comfort zone" and start being about God's business, one of the ways I did this was to joine the choir at Rutledge. Kevin was the inmate choir director. He had an amazing voice and I found out that prior to his incarceration he was the minister of music at his church. As I had been a inmate counselor at the other prisons I'd been in, Kevin pretty much ran the inmate affairs at Rutledge when I first got there. He had favor with all the staff and inmates in the prison and was known as a true Christian. Kevin ministered the Gospel to any and all, inmates and staff alike. I had never before seen an entire prison staff, with only a few exceptions trust and depend on an inmate as they did Kevin. The staffs were actually bringing their family concerns to Kevin for prayer and spiritual advice. Kevin prayed as he sang, with power and with results. There were not too many worship services where someone did not give their life to God: the tears flowed freely and without shame as this brother song or preached. It was Kevin who brought out the story teller in me to the prison multitudes instead of just the individuals and small groups I was speaking to; it was Kevin who first convinced me that I was not just a "speaker" but a called and anointed minister of the Gospel; It was he who had God's favor on his life that convinced the warden to use me to speak with and to the youth in the community. This brother was true and real in his relationship with God. Kevin was one of the many angels that God put in my path to hold me up and keep my feet aimed in the right direction.

> "He replied, "I have been very zealous for the Lord God Almighty. The Israelites have rejected your covenant, torn down your altars, and put your prophets to death with the sword. I am the only one left, and now they are trying to kill me too." "…Yet I reserve seven thousand in Israel—all whose knees have not bowed down to Baal and whose mouths have not kissed him." 1 King 19:14, 18 (NIV)

I stated earlier that "I felt as if I was the only one in this whole prison system that was actually trying to get right with God. It was as if none of the other inmates knew or cared anything about God." God showed me just how wrong I was when I arrived in Rutledge. I'd venture to guess that over seventy percent of this prison were devout Christians or at least people either trying to live the Christian life or pretending to. Most of the others were Jehovah Witnesses or Muslim. Kevin along with a strong Christian staff, unlike at any other institution I had been in, motivated and encouraged the inmates to trust God. Prayer was routinely suggested when problems arose with the inmates or their families. The counselors, doctors, mental health staff and officers did not hesitate to pray with an inmate if requested to do so. As a result there was much less violence, rapes, thefts and the other problems that are common to prisons. Many inmates here were going home well before their scheduled released date; there was testimony weekly about healings and other prayer answered miracles. We even had two inmates and an outside volunteer who was healed of late stage cancers. The "power" of God that is not often seen in the Christian faith these days, even in the "free world" was very much prevalent in Rutledge State Prison. The inmates had a powerful intercessory prayer team that got together every Saturday to pray for the many prayer requests we had received throughout the week. We prayed for each request individually; name by name, issue by issue was presented to God. The power of the Holy Spirit was in this place. "But you will receive power when the Holy Spirit comes on you; and you will be my witnesses in Jerusalem, and in all Judea and Samaria, and to the ends of the earth." Acts 1:8 (NIV)

PART SIX
"IT WON'T BE LONG TILL WE'LL BE LEAVING HERE; IT WON'T BE LONG TILL WE'LL BE GOING HOME."

"You have granted me life and favor, and your care has preserved my spirit." Job 10:12 (KJV 2000)

Prior to my incarceration my sister and I used to sing a song with the lyrics "It won't be long till we'll be leaving here…" Every day during the last few years of my incarceration as I worked in the law library and many nights shinning the floors in the dorm, front hall or wardens office I song this song out loud. Half the people in the dorm that I lived in learned this song from hearing me sing it as did many of the prison staff. Throughout my life God has shown favor on me. I know that I have been called: protected, healed, delivered and lifted up because of God's favor on my life.

All of my pre-prison associates are either dead, strung out on drug, HIV positive and mostly uneducated. By allowing me, through His permissive will, to go to prison I have been protected from all of this. These years in prison was my rescue; the time for me to learn about God and to attain my own relationship with God, not depending on my mother or grandmothers relationship and prayers with him. I would be in the same situation that my previous associates had it not been for the mercy and grace of God. I often ask, why me Lord? Why was I chosen for your favor? Why am I called to minister your word? "Before I formed thee in the belly I knew thee; and before thou camest forth out of the womb I sanctified thee, *and* I ordained thee a prophet unto the nations" was where He lead me to answer this question. Jeremiah 1:5 (KJV)

In 1993 I was hospitalized with a cyst in my thyroid. Swollen lymph nodes, fever, sore and swollen throat were the resulting symptoms. After surgery for and the removal of the cyst it was discovered that I was in the beginning stages of stage one, thyroid cancer. "But He *was* wounded for our transgressions, *He was* bruised for our iniquities; the chastisement for our peace *was* upon Him, and by His stripes we are healed" Isaiah 53:5 (KJV). After my release from prison the devil would again attack my body with cancer, but God's grace is and has been sufficient, His favor has been forever on my life. "For You, O Lord, will bless the righteous; with favor You will surround him as *with* a shield." Psalm 5:12 (KJV)

> *"The thief cometh not, but for to steal, and to kill, and to destroy…" John 10:10 (KJV)*

If we as Christians would work half as hard as the devil does there would be many more Christians in the world. I've learned as a Christian that the devil never takes a break when it comes to attacking the Saints, trying to break their spirit, cause any kind of harm or even killing them. But I've also learned that the devil cannot do any more than God will allow him. One of the many tactics of the enemy (the devil), and what I believe is his most prevalent, and successful tool is fear.

My first day out of prison the enemy was on the attack trying to discourage me and steal my joy and freedom. As stated earlier Brother Ozie came to pick me up from the prison.

Even before I walked out of the prison doors the enemy attacked my mind with fear. I still could not believe that I was actually going home. I was "afraid" that something, anything was going to happen to keep me in prison. The fear only increased when I walked out the front door and didn't see Brother Ozie anywhere. Twenty-six plus years of my life, over half of my life in prison and now I stood alone outside the prison walls. As my fear rose and I begin to fret and wonder what to do next Brother Ozie pulled up. He had been there all along but had been told by the guards that he couldn't park and wait on state property but had to go across the street. He had seen me come out but it took him a minute to get there. That seemed to be the longest minute to me.

Most people will never be able to understand the mind of a person who has been institutionalized from their teenage years to their forties. I was so excited riding in that car but had such conflicting emotions of fear also. When we pulled up to a Publix grocery store my plan was to stay in the car. Brother Ozie, already on his de-institutionalization and discipleship mission ignored me and ordered me out of the car. My whole focus was on not hyperventilating and passing out. "Real stores, Lord have mercy." I just knew everybody in the place would be able to tell that I had just got out of prison. I was conscious of the clothe I was wearing and just knew that everyone knew they were given by the prison.

Bro. Ozie wanted to know what I liked and what I wanted to eat. I didn't know much, just grits. I loved grits and they rarely had them in prison. I couldn't think of much else. I was simply amazed by the size of the store itself and all the variety. In prison we had a list of about twenty items we could buy. The same list week after week, year after year, rarely changing. We wrote down on an order form the day before what we wanted and they brought it to us the next day.

After we had everything Bro. Ozie wanted and we were in the checkout line Bro. Ozie remembered something else he needed and left me in the line. He had not come back by the time our items reached the cashier. I had no idea what to do. I guess the cashier thought maybe something was wrong with me as I stood there dumb founded, sweating and in fear thinking Bro. Ozie had suddenly deserted me. This should give you an idea of a severely institutionalized person's mental state. But this was only the beginning of that first day out fears.

> *"Thou preparest a table before me in the presence of mine enemies:" Psalms 23:5 (KJV)*

I've learned over the years that no matter what the enemy throws at you God is already prepared to handle it for you and through you. God will not leave you alone in the midst of the "perceived" storm. "There hath no temptation taken you but such as is common to man: but God *is* faithful, who will not suffer you to be tempted above that ye are able; but will with the temptation also make a way to escape, that ye may be able to bear *it*." 1 Corinthians 10:13 (KJV)

When granted parole you are required to report to the parole office within seventy two hours after your release. Me and Ozie decided to get this out of the way my first day out. The first thing they do when you get to the parole office is to drug test you to see if you have been doing any drugs since your release. I failed the drug test for meth. I couldn't even tell you what meth looks like but here I am my first day out of prison back in handcuffs and being told that I'm on my way back to prison. Nobody in the parole office would listen to my objections and denials. I was called a liar and told to shut up and sit down while I waited to be taken back to the prison. They wanted to know where I had gotten to drugs on my first day out or had I taken them before I got out. But you know God always have a ram in the bush; a sacrifice for his people; a savior!

My assigned parole officer, who I had not yet meet came into the building. A young but apparently veteran of the parole business. She listened as all the other parole officers, even the chief, told her what a stupid fool I was to have spent all that time in prison and then to come into their office with drugs in my system. But "In the LORD's hand the king's heart is a stream of water that he channels toward all who please him." Proverbs 21:1 (NIV)

This parole officer, who I had never met, called me into her office, sat me down and just looked at me for several minutes. She then got up, took the handcuffs off and told me to sit back down, "not to worry nobody is going to send you back to prison today." She told her chief that she knew for a fact that I had not done any drugs. She asked me if I had a girlfriend. No. Have I ever dealt with white girls? No. She then proceeded to tell the chief and the other parole officers that if I was going to be dirty on drugs it would be marijuana not meth because in her experience only black guys who had white girlfriend or associates did meth; secondly she had read my file thoroughly and drugs didn't fit my profile nor my religious beliefs which she was sure that I was committed to.

How then did two drug tests come back positive for meth? She asked if I was taking any medication. Yes I was; Medication for high blood pressure, high cholesterol, and acid reflux. I presented the meds to her. The acid reflux medication causes false positives for meth and she seemed to be the only parole officer there who knew this. I was told not to tell the other parolees about this as they would try to use this information to get by drug test. Satan don't you know that I am a child of the King and thus "it is finished."

"A wise man will hear, and will increase learning; and a man of understanding shall attain unto wise counsels:" Proverbs 1:5 (KJV)

For the next several months I would be on a sort of house arrest in Brother Ozie's house. I had an ankle monitor on and could only leave the house during the day to look for work. I wanted to go to church so bad but had to be in the house by seven every week night and wasn't allowed to go out on the weekends. But during this time I was learning, constantly learning. It would take Brother Ozie a number of months before he could force me to give up the plastic and paper plates and "sporks." I was afraid I'd break his "real" dishes. I was like a new baby just born into a new world. I was fascinated by the internet; the television shows and even the television itself. When I was first locked up the minimum wage was $2.10 an hour; it was now seven twenty five.

Reading the Bible for hours every day and having conversations with Brother Ozie about God, life and the Bible. Learning to trust that God really had not brought me this far to leave me. I could go to bed now without sleeping fully dressed with my boots on; I didn't have to get up every two hours for "count time"; I wasn't told when to go to breakfast, lunch or dinner and after my first week in Ozie's house no one was fixing my meals for me anymore. I started getting food stamps and had to learn to buy my own food, not just ramen noodle soups, instant chili, chips, and other junk food. I had to learn to "self checkout" at the store (this was a major shock).

But God had truly blessed me: there was Ozie in my life, Mike, my mama and my parole officer. All these people and some more were teaching me and helping me.

"Behold, I send an Angel before thee, to keep thee in the way, and to bring thee into the place which I have prepared." Exodus 23:20 (KJV)

As soon as I asked God to open the door of opportunity for me so that I could find a job He did. My second week out I was hired on with the construction company that my father had worked with for over forty years. I was given a desk and an office in accounting and filing. Without question I was assigned the duty of logging all the payroll checks into the computer and in the proper file folders and then send them out to the superintendents. Millions of dollars were passing through my hands daily. A few weeks later I was also asked and assigned as the building custodian and was working from six in the morning to nine every night. I was given keys to the building and my own alarm access code.

I passed my driver's license test on the first try and God blessed me with a car in my first month out. I still wasn't allowed to go anywhere except for work. I got lost everywhere I went it seemed.

One of my nephews brought three young ladies over to Brother Ozie's house while he was at work one night with the intent of "getting you laid Unc." I had to threaten to call the police on him to get him to leave. The devil was set on causing me to fall and he didn't care who or how he accomplished his mission. My brothers tried to set me up by getting me drunk so they too could get me "laid" with one of their friends. It was unbelievable to them that I didn't drink alcohol nor had any desire to do so. God in His mercy and grace had kept me from all of these addictions. When I refused to sleep with any of the women presented to me I was labeled as being gay. Even my own mother asked me this question. People didn't realize and many still don't realize the extent of my dedication to God. To the best of my ability I intend to honor, obey and worship God in every aspect of my life with my every breath.

PART SEVEN
RESTORATIONS

"And I will restore to you the years that the locust hath eaten, the cankerworm, and the caterpillar, and the palmerworm, my great army which I sent among you." Joel 2:25 (KJV)

My son was a young man with three kids when I was released from prison. For those first few months I was out he became my right hand. He taught me how to get from place to place without getting lost; he taught me how to ride the public transportation system; he took me to my first Braves baseball game, and he introduced my beautiful grand babies into my life. About the happiest moments of my life was spent with him during my first year out. When God started opening up the doors of opportunity for me to preach the gospel, particularly in other cities and states it was my son who made sure that I got there and back. During the first opportunity I had to preach, in Phoenix City Alabama, my son came with tears in his eyes to give his life to God. But my son had some serious and deep issues to deal with and that even today he is still dealing with. Like many others in my family he had an addiction, cocaine. When he told me of this addiction I naively felt that God would immediately remove this desire from him as he had the cigarettes with me. It was not to be so. It took much prayer and a stint of me secretly and forcibly isolating him from the world for several weeks under the pretense that I needed him to accompany me on a out of town trip. He was straight for a while but eventually fell back into it.

Finally, I had no choice but to trust God and put my son and his situation in God's hand. I had to force and train myself to not keep interfering with what God was doing. I had to recognized that only God could heal him and that he may have to go "through something" to be fully delivered. I feel guilty often now as I believe that had I removed myself and allowed God to work this out from the beginning the deliverance would have been quicker and easier. My son is now following in my foot steps: he's in prison, though, not for murder thank God. I have all the confidence in the world that God is working on and working with my child and am going to bring him into a relationship with Him.

> "Ask, and it shall be given you; seek, and ye shall find; knock, and it shall be opened unto you:" Matthew 7:7 (KJV)

    We often ask God for things and in His love and in His "permissive" will He will give us our hearts desire. I wanted a wife and a particular wife at that. One of the psychological effects so much time in prison has on a person is a mental death or mental "stuck-ness" whereas you see things in your mind the same way they were when you get out of prison as they were when you went in. In your mind a person who was sixteen when you went into prison is still sixteen when you get out. When I was released from prison my mind was still stuck on the images and feelings I had of and for people before I went in. I wanted and asked God to let me find and meet with the same girl friend that I had been in love with for many years before I went to prison (Not my sons mother).

My sister ran into her on the bus in downtown Atlanta and gave her my phone number. As I stated earlier I do not believe in accident or co-incident. I asked and God answered.

We met for dinner; re-introduced ourselves and when I heard that she was not nor had she ever been married I felt that God had answered my prayers. The following year after we met we were married. I had told nobody, not even Ozie about this nor had I asked the advice or prayers of any of the saints. In fact I have made a number of decisions without asking God about them and only realized this after it was brought to my attention by Bro. Ozie. One of Ozie's favorite sayings to me when he noticed I was making decisions without seeking God or godly counsel is "I see you joining the rat race out here." It took me a while to realize that he was telling me that I was doing as the rest of the world seemed to be doing. "Join the crowd." Doing what I wanted; doing it my way, the way of the world. Again, thank God for His mercy and Grace.

Saying, Father, if thou be willing, remove this cup from me: nevertheless not my will, but thine, be done. Luke 22:42 (KJV)

"Nevertheless not my will, but thine, be done" is a prayer that I don't think many of us really think about. I spoke earlier about God granting us our prayers as part of His permissive will. I also cited the scripture where God promised "And I will restore to you the years that the locust hath eaten, the cankerworm, and the caterpillar, and the palmerworm, my great army which I sent among you" (Joel 2:25, KJV). I have discovered though that God's permissive will is not the will He intends for us even though we seem to relish in this way as it tends to favor what we want for our lives over what God has planned."For my thoughts are not your thoughts, neither are your ways my ways," declares the Lord." Jesus taught the disciples to pray "thou will be done on earth as it is in heaven." We should seek Gods will in and over our lives here on earth just as His will for our lives is done in heaven, His perfect will.

The Apostle Paul said that he was "forgetting what is behind and straining toward what is ahead" (Philippians 3:13). So how is that we crave for God to "restore" to us what was taken in the past? This is just what I did, out of fear, of new beginnings, when I asked God to "restore" to me things, people, from my past. I did not think of consequences or whether this person was the same person they were when I went into prison. All I was thinking was that God had promised to "restore" and I held Him to that promise not realizing that the restoration would have and should have been something new. I am talking about my wife or ex-wife now. Our marriage lasted for about four years and there were times during those four years that I wished I was back in prison. I was not ready for marriage and when I did get married we were "unequally yoked" as I was preaching and in church somewhere most of the time and she was on another level. Our break up was not the fault of any one thing other than the fact that we had nothing in common, I had changed a lot but she was still the beautiful young girl of the world that I had left when I went to prison. "Therefore if any man *be* in Christ, *he is* a new creature: old things are passed away; behold, all things are become new" (2 Corinthians 5:17). As I reflect back on what I thought was "restoration" and the Prophet Job, I began to realize that when God restored Job, all of the restoration was new. Job's original sons and daughters were dead; his old wealth was gone. In fact all the "old was gone, all things became new."

Brethren, if a man be overtaken in a fault, ye which are spiritual, restore such an one in the spirit of meekness: considering thyself, lest thou also be tempted. Bear ye one another's burdens, and so. fulfill the law of Christ. Galatians 6:1-2 (KJV)

Bro. Ozie was my guide, my counselor, the person I was accountable to in order to stay on the right track. I have come to realize that it doesn't matter how strong you are in the Lord you still need someone to be accountable to. However, I didn't always ask or follow his advice. In some situations I had no choice in seeking or listening to his advice. After staying at Ozie's house the first eight months after my release from prison I was instructed by my parole officer that it was time for me to move on and try to live by myself.

One of the most difficult things for an ex- convict is finding work. No one wants to hire a person with a prison record, thank God that this was not a difficulty for me. Another of the nearly impossible things that ex-cons face is that most apartment applications ask if you have a criminal conviction and if so you are denied. Several apartment complex's I applied to actually told me that they had no problem with my criminal background and once they got my application fee, usually fifty dollars or more, I was told that I was denied and the application fee is non-refundable.

This time, afraid that I would jeopardize my parole, I did ask God to help me and I found a good, inexpensive, efficiency apartment. But, there are a number of other issues that I acted alone on when I shouldn't have. For example, I was blessed with a little car. It ran good, saved on gas and was paid for.

"Pride goes before destruction, a haughty spirit before a fall." Proverbs 16:18 (KJV)

I was preaching nearly every night of the week and on weekends and as Bro. Ozie used to say I was "in high demand." From South Georgia, Florida, Alabama, and Texas I was being asked to speak. The churches and organizations that invited me were paying all of my expenses and giving me generous offerings. I decided that as a preacher I needed to look better in something more than the twenty year old dent up Camry I had. I felt like I was making good enough money from my job and from speaking that I could afford a better looking car. I did seek Bro. Ozie's counsel on this issue as I thought that he would surely see the reasoning behind why I needed a better car. I was representing God, I had to look good. But Bro. Ozie advised against it and explained that he didn't' think I was ready for the responsibility and that I needed to concentrate on saving money for when I had to live on my own. As always though, he told me to pray about it and seek God's counsel. The next day I bought a new car; a car that decided after only one day that it would turn off on its own whenever it was ready. The car was a lemon and I had traded my Camry in as a down payment for it. I was also paying a four hundred dollar a month car note and couldn't even drive back and forth to work. After arguing with the dealership for a few days I decided that even if I couldn't get my old car back I was not going to keep paying this car note for a car that I couldn't drive. I took the car back to the lot and left it there. It would take yet another lesson like this before I learned. I've had a Jaguar, Mercedes, and another Toyota Camry, though a much newer one. Now I'm happy, and satisfied with my twenty-plus year old Camry that is paid for. I've learned that God will not bless you with more until and unless you are grateful for what He has already blessed you with.

"God is faithful. by whom ye were called unto the fellowship of his Son, Jesus Christ our Lord." I Corinthians 1:9 (KJV)

God is so true and amazing in His faithfulness. Throughout all of the times I was not faithful, tried to go it on my own, wouldn't listen, God was and is true to His faithfulness. He has held me up, kept me in His arms of love and protected me from my own ignorance and sometimes stupidity.

I've had a bout with colon cancer and God brought me through; I was brought up in a legal matter with some relatives of mine and God brought me through; started a business and bought a house, and much more but through the good and the bad God has stood true and faithful to this servant.

I've come to discover that life is such a struggle out here in this "free-world." Things you come to take for granted in prison, things that you never think about such as having to pay bills. In prison there was no rent, gas or light bill. You couldn't have a cell phone in prison and when you were allowed to use the phone you're family paid for it. Buying food and toiletries, simple things like toilet paper, tooth paste, soap. Yeah some of these things you bought in prison but if you didn't have the money the state supplied you with their version. (Of course their version of these things was rough and nasty to encourage you to buy them yourselves). In prison there were no serious relationship problems and after the first couple of years all your outside relationships were usually over and any relationships you established in prison were either illegal (with a staff member) or homosexual.

 One of the biggest problems with prison is the redundancy; daily the same thing day in and out. For many years I dealt with this by gambling, playing poker, until finally it too became a bore. " Do not conform to the pattern of this world, but be transformed by the renewing of your mind. Then you will be able to test and approve what God's will is, his good, pleasing and perfect will." Romans 12:2 (NIV). One of the key ingredients to salvation is to be "transformed by the renewing of your mind." Your mind will not miraculously or magically transform itself. "Transformation" comes about through the Word of God, prayer and being in the presence of other saints. I was reading my Bible daily throughout the time I was in prison. I soon begin praying every night and every morning when I woke up. Finally, as Brother Ozie had advised I started to "come out of my comfort zone", being an island or "closet Christian." I used to be one of those Christian that felt that I had no need to go to church to be a Christian. I could have church right there in the dorm myself by listening to the radio and watching television church services. But I later learned that where much is given much is required." Luke 12:48 (NIV)

God had entrusted me with His word and knowledge and understanding of His word; also the ability to communicate His word to others in a special way; and He had given me the trust and favor of those in authority. I learned that I could not forsake the Church, which is in deed and in fact the body of Christ. "Not forsaking the assembling of ourselves together, as the manner of some is; but exhorting one another: and so much the more, as ye see the day approaching." Hebrews 10:25 (KJV)

"For as the body is one, and hath many members, and all the members of that one body, being many, are one body: so also is Christ. For by one Spirit are we all baptized into one body, whether we be Jews or Gentiles, whether we be bond or free; and have been all made to drink into one Spirit. For the body is not one member, but many." (1Corinthians 12:12-14)

Community Church of God, "A Real Church for Real People." This was Brother Ozie's Church and I felt that it was also my church even while I was still in prison. Two people originally caught my attention at "Community": Ozie was one. I had once preached a sermon to a group of churches that visited the prison on being Ambassador's for Christ." Ozie was an Ambassador for Christ but he was also an ambassador for Community Church; and

I had also met the Pastor of Community, not personally, but through his writings in the church news letter, Pastor Rudolph Smith. It was my opinion that if a church produced such people as Ozie and had such a wise leader as Pastor Rudolph Smith then it had to be a true Church of God. "Now then we are ambassadors for Christ, as though God did beseech you by us: we pray you in Christ's stead, be ye reconciled to God." 2 Corinthians 5:20 (KJV)

However, as my release day drew closer my mind begin to wonder if maybe I was suppose to join the church I was raised in. It was the church that had taught me the same Bible that had carried me all these years in prison. A part of my mind was still afraid that I was dishing God by rejecting this church. Here it is almost three decades later and the fear that had been instilled in me all those years ago was still there. Even if I didn't join this church, the one I was raised in, I made it up in my mind that I was going to visit and see where the Lord led me.

When I first visited Community though, I knew this was the place God wanted me to be. The teaching and preaching were in line with God's word; the fellowship showed such love that it brought me to tears (though nearly anything brought me to tears in those days); but it was the minister of music, Pastor Antonio that really drew me. Not just his music but his spirit, his family, his life as a whole as far as l could see was anointed.

Pastor Antonio was eventually called to start his own congregation but it is at Community that God had planted me, showed me love from its members, and supported me even though I think that some there doubted me. Even when Pastor Antonio left I never considered following him as I've learned that it is Christ that we must follow and through His faithfulness God lead me to

Community and it's at Community that I shall remain until God moves me.

When I was released from prison it was not Pastor Rudolph whose stewardship I was placed under but his son and, as always God was faithful and true in putting a shepherd in my life and over me that I could trust and who has proven to be compassionate, kind and knowledgeable, wise and caring.

He was another angel that God has sent into my life, Pastor Dr. Michael Allen Smith the son or Pastor Rudolph whom had taken over the leadership of Community when his father retired. He has encouraged me and provided me with opportunities to both minister the gospel and to learn and grow in the gospel. Pastor Michael is not only an outstanding and upstanding preacher of the gospel of Jesus Christ but he has the gift of teaching. If I begin to write the things that I have learned under his stewardship I would be writing yet another book. As I continue to run this race there is no better place for me to be, no better stewardship for me to be under than where I am now, where God has planted me.

PART EIGHT
LIVING ON THE OUTSIDE 2010 TO PRESENT (2023)

But you, keep your head in all situations, endure hardship, do the work of an evangelist, discharge all the duties of your ministry. 2Timothy 4:5

I started writing this missive back in 2014 and had thought it was finished, and this includes the conclusion that follows this particular chapter which is being written in 2023. Between the first and parts and the conclusion much has happened, though I won't even begin to try and tell it all.

However, some parts that I mentioned earlier and some I haven't mentioned I felt the need to "testify" or witness to.

I mentioned that since my release that I had colon cancer, suffice it to know that again that God is still in the miracle business and if you are a child of God His favor is on your life. From creation until Adam sinned, cancer was not something man was meant to suffer. As with many others issues both in prison and out, I believe that this cancer attack (and that's what I believe it was, an attack from the pits of hell to test and try my faith), was the devils way of trying to discourage, depress, cause fear, and move me away from my trust in God; to make all of my testimony into a lie. My mother passed in 2011 from colon cancer and in essence the devil thought that this would cause such a fear in me that I'd abandon my faith or question God. Now, know that I never lost my faith but for a short few hours only I did in fact fear and question God about this. But like King Hezekiah in the book of 2 Kings, once I turned my face to the wall and cried out to God, He gave the antidote to my fear problem and gave me peace in the midst of the storm. At that time my fear of death or the consequences of the cancer simply vanished, just like the cigarette smoking did. I knew that if it was until death that "to be absent from the body was to be present with the Lord" (2 Corinthians 5:8). As the next few days and weeks passed God pressed it on my heart that He was not through with me yet but building on my testimony resume. The cancer was removed, the treatment begun and finished and it has been over seven years cancer free now.

Prior to the cancer diagnosis I had started my own business, a U-Haul franchise and auto mechanic shop. After being diagnosed with cancer I ended up having to sell the business, and the new Mercedes I had bought to pay medical bills. I had also bought a house (you see here how God had fulfilled His promise to me to "restore everything the cankerworm had eaten") and married my childhood sweetheart. I had a weekly radio show on every Friday and had been interviewed on TV giving my testimony. Life was just one big blessing after another. But, "Dear friends, do not be surprised at the fiery ordeal that has come on you to test you, as though something strange were happening to you" (1 Peter 4:12). Over the years I have come to believe, no, to know that God allows things to happen for a reason and often we a can't understand His reasons ""For my thoughts are not your thoughts, neither are your ways my ways," declares the LORD. "As the heavens are higher than the earth, so are my ways higher than your ways and my thoughts than your thoughts" (Isaiah 55:8, 9). God was not through with me yet.

Note that I didn't mention anything about losing the house I had bought. But it was a struggle to keep it. I went over a year without paying the mortgage and everyday there was the "fear" that I'd be put out on the street (there goes that word again, fear, the main tool in the devils arsenal). I filed for bankruptcy which cleared all my other debt except for $143,000 in college debt and my mortgage. I couldn't work and filed for disability myself, thinking that because I had a degree in law that it would be nothing to it. The bank decided to try to refinance my mortgage at a lower interest rate to try to keep me in the house, but I think it was the time it took to set up this refinance that God used to save the house. By the time they had completed everything I had come to my senses, hired a law firm and been approved for disability.

Remember earlier me talking about the angels God send into our lives. Even after getting disability it was a struggle to keep my house because the mortgage took up two thirds of the disability every month, but by God's grace, Bro Ozie, sometimes my church, Mike, Mr. Helton and others came through to help keep the other bills paid, until…

Covid struck. I had been struggling all these years, thankful that God was allowing me to make it day by day, month by month, and year by year. God was still meeting all my needs, though not, I don't believe, "according to His richness in glory, but in accordance to my prayers at that time that He'll just help me make it through day by day. He was honoring both my contentment with just making it and my prayers to keep just making it. "Fret not about anything, but in everything, by prayer and supplication with thanksgiving, let your requests be made known unto God" (Philippians 4:6).

From the beginning of me committing my life to God until Covid struck, witnessing in prison, traveling and preaching, counseling and advising others there was one commandment of God that I had never honored or even thought that much about over the years. Every Sunday in church I would put whatever I thought I could afford in the collection plate. Sometimes it would be one dollar, five, ten, maybe even twenty every now and then.

As you may recall I explained earlier how the church I grew up in demanded that we pay our church dues, i.e. Sunday school dues, choir dues, youth dues, pastor rally money etc… Other than taking the youth in the church on a few trips every year, Disney world, Callaway Gardens, and conventions I never heard of the church doing anything in or for the community or anyone else outside of that church, so I was not too keen on giving money to the church thinking like most of society that all the money was going into the preachers pocket.

God used the covid virus to yet again teach me a lesson and help me grow in my faith. I was still struggling yet at the same time I would try to help others whenever or however I could often sacrificing something I needed. On two separate particular occasions my young nephew was riding with me when I stopped what I was doing to help someone else (he had been with me on numerous other occasions but these two stood out to me as a lesson from God). In the parking lot of a store a elderly lady had fallen down and people were just walking by as if not seeing her. I stopped and of course helped her, practically carrying her to her car and begging her to let me call 911. When she would accept me call for help I followed her home and made sure she got in her house ok; the second incident we were riding and I saw a overturned car at an intersection. Again cars were riding by and steering clear of the overturned car and you could see someone was inside. I stopped. Helped the lady out of the car and, gave her my coat as it was cold and raining, and waited with her until the police and ambulance arrived. My nephew asked me after we left why I helped someone I didn't know and even gave her my jacket. What has this got to do with covid and not giving to the church? Well I told my nephew what my mother had told us about not giving to someone in need and then her having to answer to God for it and if that person was using her then they had to answer to God but her conscious was clear.

After telling my nephew this at that exact same moment God brought to my attention that my reasoning for not tithing was based on the same theory. If I gave to the church and the church, pastor, or whoever, if they used these funds for anything outside of what God wanted them to use them for then it would be them who had to answer to God, but If I failed to give and the church couldn't fulfilling its calling because of my "fear" and disobedience (it was not a request that we tithe but a law, "will a man rob God?"), then it was I who would have to answer to God. And had not God Himself used the church, and those in the church, Ozie, Mike, Mr. Helton, and others to help me make it through?

When the first government payouts for covid came, before I got mine I promised God that I would start tithing. The scripture in Malachi 3:10 instructs us to bring in "all the tithes into Gods storehouse." Then it goes on to challenge us to "Test me in this," says the LORD Almighty, "and see if I will not throw open the floodgates of heaven and pour out so much blessing that there will not be room enough to store it." The key phrase in this to me at that time was "Test me in this." Still struggling as I was living only on a disability check each month, here I was permitted by the Bible itself to "test" God, so test Him I did.

I had no real "fear" of tithing from the government check I was about to receive. It was money that I had not had to depend on to survive, extra money. The lesson I had to learn was that it was not even the money I got each month that I survived on but instead it was God's grace and mercy that was seeing me through. I made a vow to God…to "test" Him. I would tithe first from the government check and for three months afterwards from my monthly check to "see if He will not throw open the floodgates of heaven and pour out so much blessing that there will not be room enough to store it." I spoke truthfully to God telling Him that I was afraid to do this, afraid that I would get further behind on everything, but if He gave me the strength I was going to stick with this for a total of four months just to see…

I had been praying the previous few months and talking to God, thanking Him for meeting all my needs, but I had become no longer content to just make it. I didn't play the lottery, though I was tempted, and I knew of no way to dig myself out of the financial situation I was in short of trying to go back to work and hustling to make more money. All kinds of ideas came to my mind during this time, but in my conversations with God I pleaded with Him to show me a way. When said start tithing was the answer it became not a on God but a test on me. Thank God I passed the test.

The second month of my tithing I received a letter stating that all of my college loans were "forgiven" due to my disability. What caught my attention was the word "forgive." Jesus paid it all, "the chastisement of our peace *was* upon him" (Isaiah 53:5).

While I was still in shock of this miracle, praising and telling everybody how good God had been to me, a few days later I heard a knock on the door. Jesus tells us that "Here I am! I stand at the door and knock. If anyone hears my voice and opens the door, I will come in and eat with that person, and they with me" (Revelations 3:20). I believe that sometimes that knock comes in the form of another one those Angels I spoke of earlier.

The knock on the door was from an angel in the form of a man, working as a real-estate agent. So that you'll know that this was indeed from God, there had been a number of real-estate agents who had been at my door and who wrote me letter nearly every day talking about they wanted to buy my house, and I had turned each away and simply thrown the letter in the trash. I was about to do the same with this one when he asked me to "just hear me out, then if you want to throw me out and I won't bother you anymore." Do to the fact that he didn't seem to be one these fast talking, what I believed were con men, I decided to hear him out, and I don't believe that this decision was totally made by me but by the Holy Spirit which gave me the patience to decide I'd hear him out.

I had bought this house in 2009 for less than seventy thousand dollars and even with the refinance I had done I owed less than half that on the house at this time. This man told me he had a client that would give $235,000 for my house. I didn't believe him. Thinking he was running a con, and just to be polite I told him that I had to pray about it and I'd get back to him, but with no actual intention of doing so. He left a bunch of paperwork with me about his company and about my house.

Over the next few days though his offer would not leave my mind and again I believe that God was willing me to listen. I called a real estate agent that I knew and asked her to check him out. While waiting on her to return my phone the man sent me an email where his offer had went up from $235,000 to $265,000 and this made me really think con game. But when my friend got back to me she informed that it was not a con, and that the man had already bought several other houses in my neighborhood for much more than they were worth. I asked her to call him and if this was real and what God wanted, for her to find me a house, in the country, that I could afford to pay cash for with what was left over from the sell. I sold the house, bought and paid for another, in the country of course (and with two acres of land). I've been at peace every since.

The whole point of this telling was that God showed me that "obedience is better than sacrifice" and that a lot of times when we think we have to sacrifice, it's not really sacrifice God is asking for but obedience, the sacrifice was made on Calvary's cross over two thousand years ago… "It is finished" (John 19:30).

There is yet one more event that has taken place in my life since I first wrote the conclusion to this missive that I'd like to witness to. Again it pertains to yet another episode of "fear." As I said earlier I think that fear is the devils number one tool in his toolbox against man. One of the biggest fears is the fear of change; the fear of beginning incarceration and being released from incarceration, a loss relationship and having to start over, any kind of unknown change. God has given some the ability to except change as an opportunity and I believe this is His will for all of us.

A few months before covid struck our pastor, Dr. Michael, and our first lady decided that God wanted them to retire. Being a double convicted criminal I didn't know how a new pastor would accept me being a minister, let alone being over the prison ministry in the church. The new pastor I'd only briefly met once and judging the book before I read it I decided nope, he wasn't the right one. Was I ever WRONG! Again! Pastor Kevin (not the Kevin from prison) has become the most influential person in my life outside of Jesus. This man has taught me stuff I never knew, some I thought I knew, and have blessed me more spiritually, emotionally, and if life period more than anyone since my mother and Bro. Ozie. He has been and is the blessings of being able to "see" how an ambassador of Christ is suppose to live. He exemplifies the scripture "So we are Christ's ambassadors; God is making his appeal through us. We speak for Christ when we plead, "Come back to God" (2 Corinthians 5:20). There may come along in the future a more influential pastor in my life but I don't believe there will ever be one more God lead, humble, and as he once put it when I needed help moving one who is not "boogie." He does not think "more highly of himself than he ought ("For I say, through the grace given unto me, to every man that is among you, not to think of himself more highly than he ought to think; but to think soberly, according as God hath dealt to every man the measure of faith" (Romans 12:3); yet he know without a doubt his place as a Kings child, "I no longer call you servants, because a servant does not know his master's business. Instead, I have called you friends, for everything that I learned from my Father I have made known to you" (John 15:15).

God has used Pastor Kevin to bring me out of a shell of being an introvert (still working on it) into a higher calling and more confident ministry that God has assigned me to. Under God's anointing and guidance through Pastor Kevin I'm learning and growing more ever day. Thank God for Angels!

PART NINE
CONCLUSION

"However, I consider my life worth nothing to me: my only aim is to finish the race and complete the task the Lord Jesus has given me, the task of testifying to the good news of God's grace." Acts 20:24 (NJV)

"God is good! It has become a saying so prevalent and, as true as it is, we have lost the true essence of just how good God is. God is better than good; just as He is infinite in His wisdom, understanding. power and love, so too is He in His goodness. His goodness is defined in His mercy and grace towards us.

The mission that God has assigned me continues. During my bout with cancer and the legal issues with some of my family my faith was tried and as always it was God's faithfulness that carried me through.

I don't know what the future holds but I do know that God still has a work for me. There are thousands in the prisons today who need the word of God brought to them. The many angels that God sent my way and still puts in my path lets me know that I too must be an angel for others; for those still behind bars; for the lonely and the broken hearted. I have been there and I am a witness of God goodness, His grace and mercy. There is a fire that burns within me that I cannot fully explain but oh how I want to just tell everybody about this great and awesome God that I serve.

"For I determined not to know anything among you save Jesus Christ and him crucified." 1 Corinthians 2:2 (KJV)

My whole life story can be summed up in the scripture "Jesus Christ and Him crucified." It doesn't matter what I've been through, or what I'm going through or may go through in the future. Jesus Christ is the center of my life. This doesn't mean that I'll never get sick again, or that I'll never have any more problems or even that I'll never fail or fall again. I know that as long as I am in this world I will have trials and tribulations... I also know, as Pastor Mike often says, "the biggest room in the universe is the room for improvement." My goal is to preach the Gospel of Jesus Christ until the day God calls me home: To let everybody know what God has done and is doing in my life, for me, with me, and through me. People must know that God is available to us all through His Son Jesus Christ and desires a personal relationship with each of us. It doesn't matter where we have been or what we have done God's mercy and grace by and through the blood of His Son means full forgiveness, redemption, pardon and life eternal with God.

In the words of our Lord, "The Spirit of the Lord is upon me, because he has anointed me to preach the Gospel to the poor. He has sent me to proclaim release to the captives, and recovery of sight to the blind. To set free those who are oppressed, to proclaim the favorable year of the Lord. And he closed the book, gave it back to the attendant and sat down; and the eyes of all in the synagogue were fixed on him. And he begin to say to them, today this Scripture is fulfilled in your hearing." Luke 4:18-21 (NIV)

"May God add a blessing to the reading of His Word."

www.ingramcontent.com/pod-product-compliance
Ingram Content Group UK Ltd.
Pitfield, Milton Keynes, MK11 3LW, UK
UKHW021326180426
11947UKWH00017B/1457

9 781312 441576